Level 1 Certificate for IT Users
for City & Guilds

Databases

for Office XP

Level
1

Susan Ward

Endorsed by

City&
Guilds

www.heinemann.co.uk
✓ Free online support
✓ Useful weblinks
✓ 24 hour online ordering

01865 888058

Heinemann Educational Publishers
Halley Court, Jordan Hill, Oxford, OX2 8EJ
Part of Harcourt Education

Heinemann is a registered trademark of Harcourt Education Ltd

First published in 2004
2006   2005
10   9   8   7   6   5   4   3   2

A catalogue record for this book is available from the British Library on request.

10-digit ISBN: 0 435462 72 5
13-digit ISBN: 978 0 435462 72 7

Typeset by Techset Ltd, Gateshead
Printed and bound in UK by Thomson Litho Ltd

Tel: 01865 888058 www.heinemann.co.uk

Contents

Introduction

City & Guilds e-Quals is an exciting new range of IT qualifications developed with leading industry experts. These comprehensive, progressive awards cover everything from getting to grips with basic IT to gaining the latest professional skills.

The range consists of both user and practitioner qualifications. User qualifications (Levels 1–3) are ideal for those who use IT as part of their job or in life generally, while Practitioner qualifications (Levels 2–3) have been developed for those who need to boost their professional skills in, for example, networking or software development.

e-Quals boasts on-line testing and a dedicated website with news and support materials and web-based training. The qualifications reflect industry standards and meet the requirements of the National Qualifications Framework.

With e-Quals you will not only develop your expertise, you will gain a qualification that is recognised by employers all over the world.

The database unit is organised into five outcomes. You will learn to:

- create and maintain database storage locations
- create a simple database
- maintain a simple database
- carry out single condition searches on a database
- produce hard copy output.

You do not need any previous experience of using databases. You will learn the practical skills and the knowledge to go with them. This book covers all the learning points within the outcomes. The outcomes matching guide, near the end of the book, gives the outcomes in full and relates each learning point to the section of the book where it is covered.

Your tutor will give you a copy of the outcomes, so that you can sign and date each learning point as you master the skills and knowledge.

There are five main sections in this book. Each section contains information and practical tasks. There is a detailed method to guide you when you first learn to carry out each task. There are also some hints and reminders at intervals. At the end of a section you will have a chance to practise your skills, check your knowledge, or both. Consolidation exercises provide further practice. A sixth section provides practice assignments which cover a range of skills and are designed to be similar in style to the City & Guilds assignment for the unit. To make the most of the book, you should start at the beginning and work through the sections in order. Later sections use the databases that are created in earlier sections.

At the end of the book there are some solutions to the skills practice and check your knowledge questions. There is also a quick reference guide giving alternative methods of carrying out common tasks.

In order to give detailed methods for each task it is necessary to refer to a specific database application, though the City & Guilds unit is not specific and can be completed using any database application. This book refers to Microsoft Access 2002, which is the database application in the more complete versions of the Microsoft Office XP suite.

You will learn to

- Identify common database terms: database, table, field, record
- Access the database software from an operating system environment
- Create a suitably named directory in which to store the data files/tables
- Create a new database from a defined database structure
- Identify data types: character or text, numeric, date, currency
- Save the database
- Print all the records in a table/file including all the fields
- Exit the database software ensuring all data files/tables have been saved to an appropriate location

Information

Databases and database software

A **database** is a collection of organised data. It can be paper based, such as a card index file, or it can be on a computer. Computerised databases need software to manage them, and make the data easy to store and use.

Software is the name for computer programs. Microsoft Access is a software **application** for producing and using databases. It is also known as a database package or a database management system. It is part of the Microsoft Office suite of software. There are other database applications, such as Lotus Approach, which are used in a similar way.

Databases are widely used by organisations to store large amounts of data. The database application allows people to search quickly through the database and select the data they need. This ability to find the right data quickly makes database applications an important tool in business, government and elsewhere.

Many databases contain information about individual people. Think about the organisations that hold information about you. They may include your bank or building society, your employer, the Inland Revenue, your doctor or hospital, insurance companies, credit card companies, mail order companies, any organisations you belong to, such as the AA, any charities you donate to, and so on. You could add to the list.

Organisations that hold personal information about living people generally have to register under the Data Protection Act and abide by its principles for gathering and storing data.   →

Database terms

There are different types of database. We shall use the type that stores its information in a **table**. A table can be shown as a grid of rows and columns.

Surname	Forename	Title	Location	Start date	Full time	Salary	Payroll No
Ford	Harold	Cashier	Oxford	01/03/98	FALSE	10500	302
Adkins	Nick	Cashier	Reading	01/06/95	FALSE	11500	303
Wheeler	Pam	IT Technician	Reading	01/04/99	TRUE	16500	304
Shah	Parveen	Manager	Newbury	01/06/85	TRUE	26000	305
Jackson	Alice	Cashier	Oxford	01/02/80	TRUE	15000	306

Table 1.1 Employees

Table 1.1 holds data about employees of a company.

Each employee has his/her own **record**, shown as a row in the table. There is a record for Harold Ford, a record for Nick Adkins and so on. The set of related records make up the table.

Each record is split into **fields**. The headings at the top of the table are the **field names**, showing the kind of data that is stored in the fields. In Harold Ford's record, one field contains his surname, Ford, one field contains his forename, Harold, and so on.

A table should hold data about only one sort of person or thing. A company would use separate tables to hold records of stock or records of orders or records of customers. A college might have a table of student records and a table of course records. A library might have a table of book records and a table of borrower records.

A database that contains only one table is called a **flat database**. The databases you will meet at Level 1 are flat databases. Access is capable of storing several tables in the same database, and linking them together to form a relational database.

When you save a database, it will be stored as a database **file**. Access stores a whole database in one file even if the database has several tables and other objects. Some other database management packages store each table in a separate file. The City & Guilds e-Quals Database unit is designed to be used with any database package, so it sometimes uses the word 'file' where Access would use the word 'table'. You will meet the words 'file', 'table', 'record' and 'field' many times as you work through this book.

Health and safety

The City & Guilds e-Quals core unit book, *IT Principles*, has a whole section on the important topic of using computers safely and without harming yourself or other people. The issues include:

- electrical safety
- the design and layout of the work area, furniture and equipment
- good working habits.

You should develop the habits of

- sitting with a good posture
- using a correct keyboarding technique
- taking regular breaks away from the computer.

Using the keyboard and the mouse

You will use a keyboard to enter data. You will already know the layout of the keyboard and the use of the main typing keys, including Shift to key in capital letters and Caps Lock to key in all letters in capitals. Check that you can find the following keys: Tab, Enter (sometimes called Return), Delete, Backspace delete.

The Tab key is used for moving on to the next typing position. You may have used it in word processing to move to the next tab position when you indent a paragraph or line up text in columns. It is also used in databases and in Windows generally to take you to the next place where you should key in text.

The Enter key is used to start a new paragraph when you are keying in text. It is also used to tell the computer system that you have finished keying in some data and want the data to be accepted. Quite often, pressing the Enter key has the same effect as clicking a button labelled OK.

The Backspace delete key is used for deleting text one character at a time to the left of the cursor. The cursor is the flashing line at the current typing position.

The Delete key can also be used for deleting text. It deletes to the right of the cursor position. The Delete key is the key to use when you want to delete anything that is not just text. Use it when you want to delete objects such as files.

Figure 1.1 Tab key

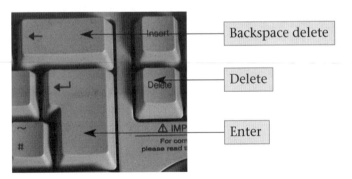

Figure 1.2 Enter and Delete keys

You will need a pointing device that lets you move a pointer on the screen and lets you click buttons to give commands. The mouse is the most usual pointing device, but there are also trackerballs, touchpads and mini joysticks. This book will refer to the mouse, but you can use any other pointing device instead. The left button is used more often than the right. The instruction 'click' or 'left click' means that you should press and release the left mouse button. 'Double click' means press and release the left mouse button quickly twice while holding the mouse still. 'Right click' means press and release the right mouse button. Some designs of mouse have a scroll wheel or additional buttons but you will not be asked to use these.

Hint:

Using the keyboard and mouse for long periods can give repetitive strain injury (RSI). To reduce the risk, take regular breaks away from the computer.

Method

This depends on the computer system you are using.

- You may be using a standalone computer that is not connected to any other computers. Switch the computer on and wait for Windows to start up. You may need to choose your own work area and perhaps enter a password.
- You may be using a computer that is linked to other computers on a network. In this case, you will probably need to log on by typing in an identification and a password. Your tutor will tell you what to do.

After a short time, the Windows desktop should appear. Your desktop will not be exactly the same as Figure 1.3 but you should be able to recognise the start button, the taskbar and some icons. There may be a window displayed, or there may not.

Microsoft Windows is the **operating system** of the computer. It is the program that controls all the parts of the computer. It lets you run other programs, such as Access, and it lets you save and manage files.

This book covers the basic Windows features that you need in order to use Access and complete the Databases unit. Other Windows features outside the scope of this book are covered in the core unit *IT Principles*.

Figure 1.3 Windows desktop

Method

1   Click with the mouse on the Start button at the bottom left of the screen.
2   A menu of options opens. Yours may look different from Figure 1.4. It depends on the programs that are installed on your computer. Select All Programs from the menu, then select Microsoft Access from the submenu by clicking with the mouse.

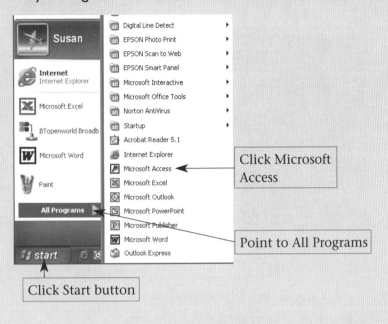

Figure 1.4 Start menu

Hint:

If you are working in a college, school or training centre then there may be more submenus before you find Microsoft Access.

Information: Files and folders

You will soon be creating a file to store a new Access database. Windows organises files by keeping them in folders. Your computer system has been set up to put new database files in a particular folder. This may be the **My Documents** folder. On a networked system, the folder may have some other name, such as **My Work**. If necessary, your tutor will tell you which folder you can use for storing files.

Folders can contain other folders as well as files. You will be creating a new folder called 'Access Databases' inside your existing My Documents or My Work folder. This Access Database folder is where you will store your new database file.

The word 'folder' was introduced with recent versions of Microsoft Windows. Older versions of Windows used the word 'directory' or 'subdirectory'. There are many computer installations that do not use Windows but use other operating system programs instead. The word 'directory' is commonly used with these other operating systems. 'Directory' is therefore the more general term, and may be used in City & Guilds paperwork. Just remember that a directory is the same thing as a folder.

Method

1   When Access starts, you should see a task pane with a list of options on the right of the Access window.

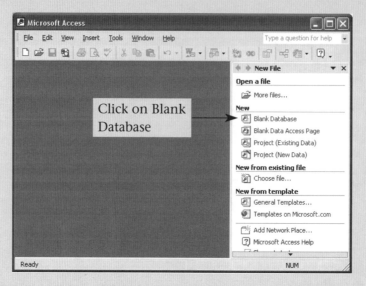

Figure 1.5 The Microsoft Access opening window with task pane

2   Find the New section and click on Blank Database.

3   The File New Database dialogue box opens.

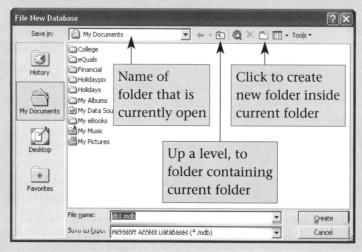

Figure 1.6 File New Database dialogue box

At the top of the dialogue box is a box labelled Save in:. This box shows the name of the folder that is open at the moment. This may be the My Documents folder as shown. If you are in a college, school or training centre then it may be some other folder.

Task 1.4 — Create a new folder to store your database files

Method

1. There are two yellow folder buttons on the toolbar at the top of the dialogue box. Point your mouse at the right-hand folder button. Hold the mouse still for a few seconds, and a label should appear saying 'Create New Folder'. This shows that you have the correct button.
2. Click the Create New Folder button.
3. A small dialogue box appears, asking you to key in the name of your new folder. Key in **Access Databases** and click OK.
4. The name of your new folder, Access Databases, should now appear in the Save in: box at the top of the dialogue box. Your Access Databases folder is inside the existing folder.

Hint:

The older and more general name for a folder is a **directory**.

Task 1.5 — Navigate to a higher level folder and back

Method

1. The File New Database dialogue box should still be on the screen. Point the mouse to the left-hand yellow folder button near the top of the dialogue box. Hold the mouse still, and a label should appear saying 'Up One Level'.
2. Click on the Up One Level button. The original folder name, e.g. My Documents, should show in the Save in: box.
3. The central part of the dialogue box is for showing a list of all the files and folders inside the current folder. This list should now contain the Access Databases folder that you created. Figure 1.7 shows part of the dialogue box at this stage.

Hint:

When you double click on a folder or file to open it, point the mouse at the little icon next to the name, not at the name itself. If you double click too slowly on the icon then nothing will happen, and you can try again. If you point to the name and double click too slowly, then the system may detect two single clicks. It will then select the folder or file name so that you can change the name. This is not what you want.

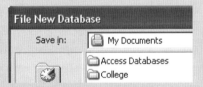

Figure 1.7 Access Databases folder inside dialogue box

4. Double click on the Access Databases folder to open it. The Access Databases name should appear in the Save in: box, and the central part of the dialogue box should be empty.

Remember:

Directory is another name for a folder.

Task 1.6 — Name and save your new database file

Method

1   Look at the File name box near the bottom of the dialogue box. It probably contains the name db1.mdb. Access calls new database files db1.mdb, db2.mdb, etc. You will give files more meaningful names.

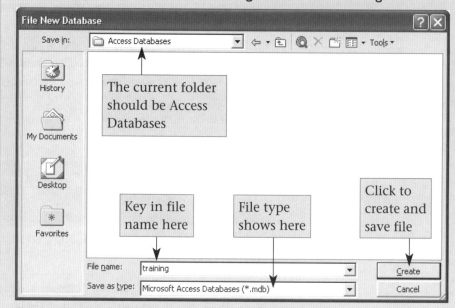

The current folder should be Access Databases

Key in file name here

File type shows here

Click to create and save file

Figure 1.8 File New Database dialogue box creating training file

2   Click into the File name box and delete any existing text. Key in **training**.
3   Look at the box labelled Save as type. This shows that your file will be saved as a Microsoft Access database file. Leave this box unchanged.
4   Click the Create button to create and save the new file.

Information: Saving to disk

While you are working, anything you key in and any changes you make are held in the computer's **main memory** (RAM). This is a volatile, temporary memory. It loses all its contents when the power supply is turned off.

In order to keep your work, you must save it as a file into long-term storage. This will normally be on a **hard disk**. On a standalone computer your files are saved on a hard disk hidden inside the main computer unit. If you are on a networked computer then your files are probably saved on a hard disk on a central computer. It is also possible to save files on a removable **floppy disk**. Your tutor will tell you if you need to use floppy disks.

You may have used word processing or spreadsheet applications where you can do a large amount of work and save it afterwards. Access forces you to save your database file before you do any work on it. This is a useful precaution to prevent loss of work if there is a power cut or a system crash.

Information: File names and file types

Every file must have a name. The main part of the name is followed by a dot and three characters called the **extension**. The extension tells the computer system what kind of data is stored in the file. Access saves its database files with the extension **.mdb**.

You can choose the main part of the name. It should remind you what is in the file. Modern computer systems allow long file names that can contain letters, numbers and spaces. Some punctuation marks are allowed but others are not. You may find it simpler to avoid using punctuation marks in file names. Some older systems allowed only 8 characters with no spaces.

When you saved your training database file, you gave it the name training. Access automatically added the extension .mdb. The full name of your database file is therefore training.mdb.

Information: The Access and database windows

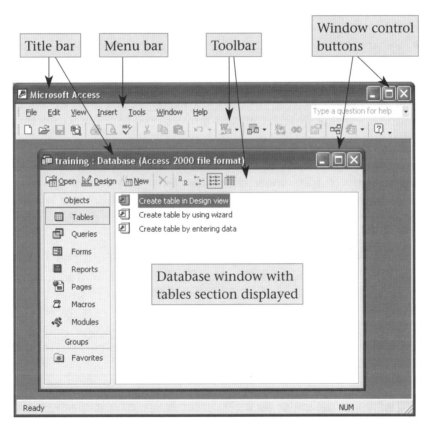

Figure 1.9 Access and database windows

On the screen you should see two windows, one inside the other, similar to Figure 1.9. The outer window belongs to Access itself. The inner window belongs to your database.

Only one window?

If you only see one window then look at its top right-hand corner.
If you see two rows of buttons looking like Figure 1.10
then click on the middle button of the lower row.
You should now see two windows.

Figure 1.10 Control buttons for two windows

The Access window

The outer window belongs to Access.

1 There is a title bar showing the name of the application, Microsoft Access.

2 There are three window control buttons at the right-hand end of the title bar. On the left is the Minimise button. On the right is the Close button. The middle button may be a Maximise button or a Restore button.

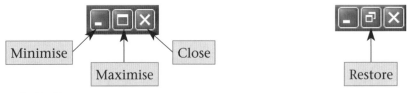

Figure 1.11 Window control buttons

Click on the Minimise button of the Access window. The Access window shrinks down to a button on the taskbar at the bottom of the screen. The button is labelled Microsoft Access and shows a key. Click on this button to bring the window back.

The Maximise button makes the window fill the screen. When the window is maximised, the Maximise button turns into a Restore button and will restore the window to an intermediate size. Click on the button a few times to maximise and restore the window. Leave the window maximised so that you have plenty of working space.

Do **not** click the close button at this stage. It would close the window, shutting down Access.

3 There is a menu bar with a row of menu names: File, Edit, View etc.
Click on File. The drop down menu should show, giving a list of options.
Click on File again to close the drop down list. You can also close the drop down list by clicking anywhere in the main part of the Access window.
Click on some of the other menu names to open and close the other drop down lists.

4 There is a toolbar with a row of buttons. Point the mouse to each button in turn without clicking, and hold it still for a few seconds. A label should appear to show the purpose of the button. Toolbar buttons give quick shortcuts to the more common features of Access.

5 At the bottom of the Access window is the status bar. It should display the word 'Ready' at the left-hand end.

Database window

The inner window is the database window.

1 There is a title bar showing the database name, training: Database. On the right are three window control buttons. Do not maximise this window. Do not use the Close button at this stage. The training database would close, but the Access window would still be open.

2 There is a toolbar with a row of buttons. You can point the mouse to the buttons and show the labels as you did with the Access window's toolbar.

3 There is an area to the left, with a set of buttons listing database objects. You will be using two types of objects: Tables and Queries. The Tables button should look as if it is pressed in, and is highlighted in blue.

4 There is a central area giving some options for creating tables. When you create a table, its name will be listed in this area.

5 Click on the Queries button. The central area now gives options for creating queries. When you create a query, its name will be listed there.

6 Click on the Tables button to return to the tables section of the database window.

Information: Data types – character or text, numeric, date and currency

You have a database file called training, but it is empty. You will create a table inside this database file. The table will be used to store data about training courses. Before you enter any data, you need to set up a table structure to hold the data. This involves setting up field names, setting the type of data to be stored in each field, and setting the sizes of the fields.

The table structure will be as follows:

Field name	Data type	Field size or format
Course Name	Text (character)	40
Location	Text (character)	30
Date	Date/Time	Short Date
Price	Currency	2 decimal places
Sessions	Number	Integer
Course Code	Text (character)	10

Table 1.2 Structure of the Training Courses table

The Course Name field will contain data entries for the names of the training courses, such as 'Introducing your PC'. The entries will consist of text and may include letters, numbers and punctuation marks. The data type must be **text**, sometimes known as character. For a text field, the field size is the number of characters the field can hold. This size should be chosen so that all possible data entries will fit into the field. The size of 40 was chosen because no course will have a name of more than 40 characters.

The Location field will hold the name of the city where the training course will be held. This field must also have a data type of text. The size of 30 characters should be more than enough for any city name.

The Date field will hold the date of the course. Access provides a special **date/time** type. Dates can be displayed in different ways. Short date displays the date in numbers, e.g. 04/09/02.

The Price field will hold the price of the course, given in pounds and pence. Typical prices might be £255.50 or £425.75. Access provides a **currency** type for storing sums of money. The display can show the £ sign and two decimal places so that the pence are shown.

The Sessions field will hold the number of sessions in each course. This will be a small whole number. Access provides a variety of **number** types. Integer or Long Integer are suitable for storing whole numbers.

The Course Code field will store codes such as 2345 or 3872a. Since some of the codes contain letters, the text type is needed. No code will have more than 10 characters, so we can choose a size of 10.

Task 1.7	Create a new database table from a defined database structure

Method

1 The Access and database windows should be showing on the screen. The Tables button should be pressed in so that the Tables section is displayed, as in Figure 1.9. The window offers three ways of creating a table.

2 Double click on Create Table in Design View. The Table design window should open.

3 Under Field Name, key in **Course Name**. Press the Tab key on the keyboard to move to the next box. The Table design window should then look like Figure 1.12.

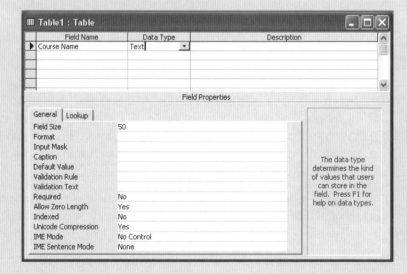

Figure 1.12 Table design window

4 The data type is shown as Text. Text is the **default** data type. The type will be Text unless you choose something different. Text is the correct data type for the Course Name field, so there is no need to change it.

5 Look at the field properties in the lower part of the window. Field size is given as 50. This is the default size. Click into the box and change 50 to 40.

6   Click back into the top part of the window, into the Description column of the Course Name field. It is not essential to put in a description, but it can be very helpful if the content of the field is not obvious from the field name.

7   Key in **Name of training course** in the Description column.

8   Press Tab to move to the second row.

9   Key in the field name **Location**, and press Tab.

10   Leave the data type as Text.

11   In the Field Properties section in the lower part of the window, change the Field size to 30.

12   In the Description column, key in **Town or City**. Press Tab.

13   In the third row, key in the field name **Date**. Press Tab to move to the Data Type column.

14   Click the little arrow in the Data Type column to show the drop down list of data types. See Figure 1.13. Click on Date/Time to select it from the list.

Hint:

You need to move to the Data Type column, otherwise the little arrow for the drop down list will not show.

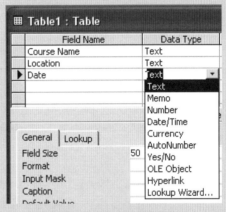

Figure 1.13 Selecting a data type

15   Look at the field properties for the Date field. The properties are not the same as the Text field properties. Click into the Format box to show an arrow, then click the arrow to show the drop down list. Figure 1.14 shows part of the Table design window with the list displayed.

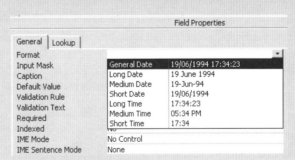

Figure 1.14 Choosing a date format

16   The list shows the different ways of displaying dates and times. Click on Short Date to select it from the list.

17   Back in the top part of the window, key in a description for the field: **Start date of course**.

18   Key in the fourth field name: **Price**.

19   In the Data Type column, click the arrow to show the drop down list. Select Currency.

20   There is no need to change any field properties. By default, the currency data type will show a £ sign and 2 decimal places.

21   Key in a description for the field: **Price of course**.

22   Key in the fifth field name: **Sessions**.

23   In the Data Type column, click the arrow to show the drop down list. Select Number.

24   Go to the Field Properties for the Sessions field. Click into the Format box to show an arrow, then click the arrow to show the drop down list. Figure 1.15 shows part of the Table design window with the list displayed.

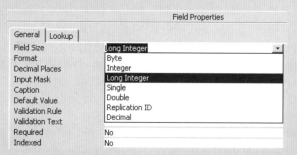

Figure 1.15 Choosing a number format

25   Integer and Long Integer types are suitable for storing whole numbers. Use Long Integer unless you are short of storage space. Single and Double types are suitable for storing numbers that have a fractional or decimal part. The Sessions field will store whole numbers, so select Long Integer from the list.

26   Key in a description for the field: **Number of sessions in course**.

27   Key in the final field name: **Course Code**.

28   Leave the data type as text, but go to the Field Properties and change the Field size to 10.

29   No description is needed for this field, but you could key in **Course Code** if you wish.

Hint:

You will need to show your name on your printouts if you are sharing a printer. You may be used to putting your name on a Word document or an Excel spreadsheet, either on the main document or in a header or footer. There is no easy way of doing this in Access. Table names are automatically printed out, so the most convenient way of printing your name is to make it part of the table name.

Task 1.8	Save the database table

Method

1   Click the Save button on the toolbar near the top of the Access window 💾

2   A small Save As box appears asking for the name of the table. Key in the table name **Training Courses (your name)**. Put your own name in the brackets.

3   Click OK.

4   A message will appear saying 'There is no primary key defined'. It will offer to create a primary key for you. Click the **No** button. Primary keys will be introduced later, but you do not need to create one at the moment.

5   The table design is saved. Look at the title bar of the Table design window. The name of the table should be displayed.

Task 1.9 — Switch between Design and Datasheet views of a table

Access provides two different ways of looking at a table. **Design view** shows the structure of the table. It shows field names, data types, field sizes and other properties of the fields. It does not show any of the data stored in the table. **Datasheet view** shows the contents of the table. It shows the grid of rows and columns containing the data. Each row contains one record. Records are split into fields and each column has a field name as its heading.

Method

1   Find and click the View button at the left of the toolbar in the Access window. Click the button itself rather than the arrow beside it.
2   You switch from the Design view of the table to the Datasheet view. This is the view that shows the contents of the table. At the moment the table is empty. There are no records. The field names are displayed as column headings. See Figure 1.16.

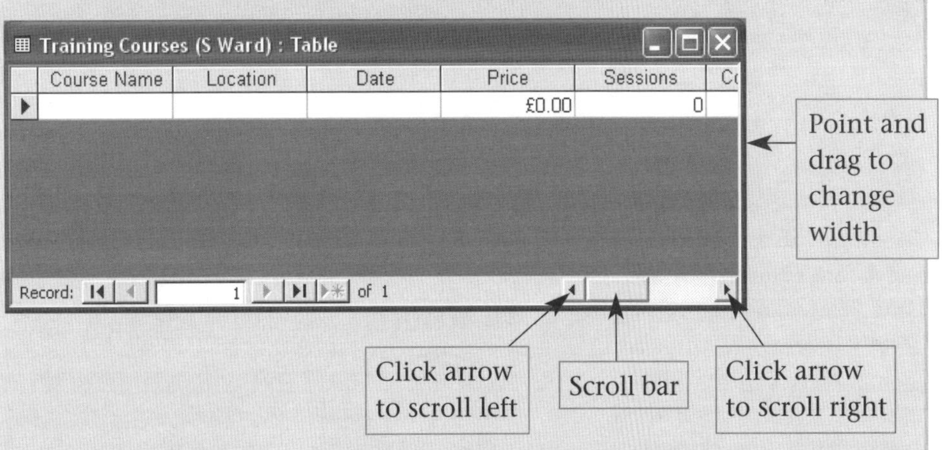

Figure 1.16 Datasheet view of the empty Training Courses table

3   The window in Figure 1.16 is not big enough to show the Course Code field. To see the missing field, use the scroll bar at the bottom of the window. Click on the right arrow to scroll to the right until the field appears. Click on the left arrow to scroll back to the left.
4   Make the window wider by pointing the mouse to the right-hand border of the window so that the mouse pointer shows as a double-headed arrow. Hold down the left mouse button and drag the mouse to the right until the window is big enough to show all the fields. Release the mouse button.
5   Find the View button at the left of the toolbar in the Access window. This button changed its appearance when you switched to Datasheet view. Click the View button to switch to Design view.
6   Click again to switch to Datasheet view. You will often switch between these two views of a table.

Hint:

Even if your window is already wide enough to show all the fields, make sure that you know how to change the width of a window and how to use a scroll bar. No scroll bar? Make the window narrower and it should appear.

Method

I   Make sure that the table is in Datasheet view, and key in the following data. Do not key in the field names again. They are already there. Do not worry at this stage if the Course Name field is not wide enough to show all its contents.

Course Name	Location	Date	Price	Sessions	Course Code
PC Troubleshooting	London	12/10/02	425.50	2	704a
Introducing your PC	Liverpool	14/10/02	250.00	2	287a
Introducing the Internet	Liverpool	15/10/02	250.00	2	288a
Upgrading a PC	London	18/10/02	600.00	3	705a
Introducing your PC	Bristol	19/10/02	250.00	2	287b
Website Development	Bristol	20/10/02	350.25	1	501a
PC Troubleshooting	Liverpool	23/10/02	425.50	2	704b
Introducing the Internet	Liverpool	24/10/02	250.00	2	288b
Networking Essentials	London	27/10/02	625.75	3	417a
Introducing your PC	London	28/10/02	250.00	2	287c

Table 1.3 Data for the Training Courses table

Hint:

Use the Tab key on the keyboard to move from one field to the next. Alternatively, you can move using the Enter key. Any existing data in a field will be selected. You can just type over the existing data if it is selected. There is no need to delete it first.

Method

The Course Name field display is too narrow to show the names. The field needs to be made wider.

I   Point the mouse at the line between the Course Name and Location field names so that the mouse pointer changes to a line with arrows pointing left and right.

2   Hold down the left mouse button and drag the mouse to the right until the field is wide enough to show the names in full. Release the mouse button.

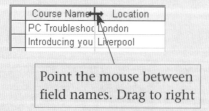

Point the mouse between field names. Drag to right

Figure 1.17 Making a field wider

Information: Field size and field width for display

When you designed the table in Design view, you set the size of the Course Name field to 40 characters. The Course Name field can store 40 characters if you key them in. If you key in more than 40 characters, the extra characters will not be stored. When you change to Datasheet view, the field is not displayed with a width of 40 characters. The field width for display can be adjusted. Changing the field width for display has no effect on the field size that you set up in the design. It does not affect the number of characters that can be stored.

It is important that you adjust the field widths so that the data entries are displayed in full. There must be no missing characters in printouts.

Hint:

When you adjust the field widths, leave a little spare space after the last character in the field. If the edge of the field is very close to the last character then it is possible for the last character to be cut off when you print the table. This can happen even if the whole of the text displays perfectly well on the screen.

Task 1.12 Print preview a table

Before printing a table, you should use the Print Preview. This shows how your table will be set out on the printed page. If your table is too big to fit on one page, it shows how the table will be split up. It also shows the automatic header that appears at the top of each page and the automatic footer that appears at the bottom. These are pre-set to show the table name, the date and the page number. You cannot change them.

Remember:

You saved the table as Training Courses and included your own name in brackets as part of the name of the table. The automatic header displays the table name. It therefore displays your name in brackets. Your name will appear at the top of the paper every time you print the table. This may seem rather a strange way of getting your name on your printouts but there is no other easy method for an Access table.

Method

1 Make sure that you can see the table on the screen in Datasheet view. Make sure that all the fields are wide enough to display all the data.
2 Click the Print Preview button on the toolbar 🔍
3 The Print Preview window appears, showing the database table as it will appear on the page. Click on the table to see an enlarged view.
4 Check to see if the whole table is displayed. Probably the last field is missing as shown in Figure 1.18.
5 Check at the bottom left of the window to see if there are additional pages. Figure 1.18 shows that there is at least one additional page. The page navigation button with the right pointing arrow is displaying its arrow in black. This shows that there is a next page. There is no previous page because the left pointing arrow is displayed in grey.
6 Click on the black 'next page' button. Page 2 displays, showing the Course Code field. This table would print on two pages, and would be difficult to read.

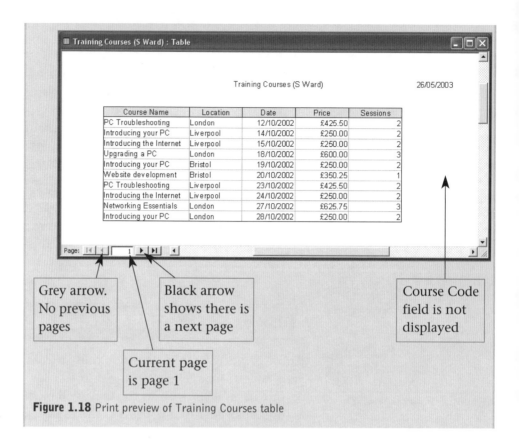

Training Courses (S Ward)   26/05/2003

Course Name	Location	Date	Price	Sessions
PC Troubleshooting	London	12/10/2002	£425.50	2
Introducing your PC	Liverpool	14/10/2002	£250.00	2
Introducing the Internet	Liverpool	15/10/2002	£250.00	2
Upgrading a PC	London	18/10/2002	£600.00	3
Introducing your PC	Bristol	19/10/2002	£250.00	2
Website development	Bristol	20/10/2002	£350.25	1
PC Troubleshooting	Liverpool	23/10/2002	£425.50	2
Introducing the Internet	Liverpool	24/10/2002	£250.00	2
Networking Essentials	London	27/10/2002	£625.75	3
Introducing your PC	London	28/10/2002	£250.00	2

Grey arrow. No previous pages

Black arrow shows there is a next page

Course Code field is not displayed

Current page is page 1

Figure 1.18 Print preview of Training Courses table

Hint:

Always print preview before you print. You will be able to spot problems, fix them, and avoid wasted printouts.

Task 1.13   Change to landscape orientation

Paper with its shorter edge across the top is in portrait orientation. If you turn the paper so that its longer edge is across the top, then it is in landscape orientation. Printing is normally done with the paper in portrait orientation, but you can choose landscape orientation for wide printouts.

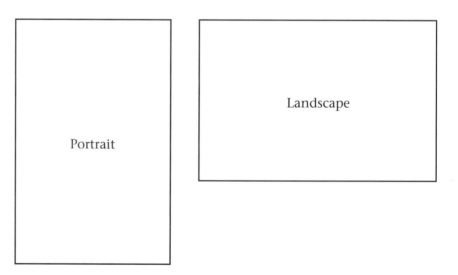

Portrait

Landscape

Figure 1.19 Portrait and landscape orientation

Method

1 Click on the File menu to display the drop down list.
2 Select Page Setup.
3 Click on the Page tab in the Page Setup dialogue box. See Figure 1.20.
4 Click in the Landscape option button to select it.
5 Click OK.
6 The print preview should now show the complete table on one page in landscape orientation.
7 Check that all data entries are shown in full with no missing characters. If any characters are missing then probably a field is not wide enough. You should make the field wider before you continue. Click the Close button Close on the toolbar to close the print preview and return to the table. Make the field wider and print preview again.

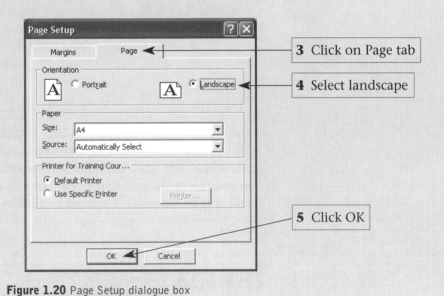

Figure 1.20 Page Setup dialogue box

Task 1.14 — Print all the records in a table/file including all the fields

Method

1 The table should be displayed on the screen in print preview with all fields showing and with all data entries shown in full.
2 Click the Print button on the toolbar
3 Check the printout carefully to make sure that all your data entries are accurate. Accuracy is very important in databases.
4 Check again to make sure that the fields were wide enough to show all characters. Occasionally a field seems to be just wide enough in print preview but is not quite wide enough for the last character to be printed.

Task 1.15 — Exit the database software ensuring all data files/tables have been saved to an appropriate location

Method

1 Click on the File menu to display the drop down list.
2 Select Close.
3 A message box should appear, asking if you want to save changes to the layout of the table. Select Yes.
4 The table closes. The database window and the Access window are still open.
5 Click on the File menu to display the drop down list.
6 Select Exit. This closes down the training database file and also the Access application. You return to your Windows desktop.

Information: Saving tables

You need to save any changes that you make to the design of a table. This includes any changes to the field widths. You do not need to save changes to the table contents. Access automatically saves each record as you move away from it to the next record. If a table needs to be saved, then Access will remind you when you close it.

Task 1.16 — Close down the computer system

Method for a standalone computer

1 Click on the Start button at the bottom left of the screen.
2 Select Turn Off Computer from the menu.
3 The Turn Off Computer dialogue box appears. Select Turn Off Computer again and click Yes.
4 Your computer may switch off by itself. If not, wait for a message saying that it is safe to switch off the computer. You can then switch off.

Method for a networked computer

1 You will need to log off. Ask your tutor about this. Logging off tells the computer system that you have finished using it. You should always log off before leaving the computer. This is a precaution to keep your work secure and private.

Remember:

Take regular breaks away from the computer.

→ Practise your skills 1: Employees

You are asked to create a database to hold information about employees. The instructions will include some reminders, but the methods will not be given in detail. Look back at the detailed methods for each task if you need to.

Instructions:

1 Start up the computer.
2 Start up Microsoft Access. **Remember**: use the Start button.
3 Choose to create a blank Access database.
4 Save your new database file in your Access Databases folder. Give the file the name **Employees**.
5 Create a table in Design view.
6 Set up the table structure as shown. There is no need to enter a description. Remember that the field size or format needs to be set in the Field Properties section in the lower part of the Table design window. Do not type the field size in the description column.

Field name	Data type	Field size or format
Surname	Text (character)	25
Initials	Text (character)	10
Title	Text (character)	20
Branch	Text (character)	20
StartDate	Date/Time	Short Date
Salary	Number	Long Integer
Payroll No	Number	Long Integer

Table 1.4 Structure of the Employees table

7 Save the table structure. Give the table the name **Employees Table**. Add your name in brackets to the table name.
8 Do not allow Access to create a primary key.
9 Change to Datasheet view. Use the Toolbar button to do this.
10 Enter records as shown:

Surname	Initials	Title	Branch	StartDate	Salary	Payroll No
Ford	H	Cashier	Exeter	01/03/98	10500	302
Adkins	N	Cashier	Reading	01/06/95	11500	303
Wheeler	P A	IT Technician	Reading	01/04/99	16500	304
Shah	P	Manager	Bradford	01/06/85	26000	305
Lancaster	K	Manager	Leeds	01/11/92	26000	306
Adams	M B	Cashier	Leeds	01/08/00	11500	307
Stephens	B	Manager	Reading	01/09/90	30000	308
Hussein	M	Cashier	Exeter	01/02/80	15000	309
Wilkins	D S	IT Technician	Exeter	01/12/99	16000	310
Watson	P	Manager	Exeter	01/03/82	28000	311
Evans	K	Cashier	Newbury	01/04/89	14600	312
Smith	T	IT Technician	Leeds	01/02/01	10000	313
Erikson	K	Cashier	Reading	01/12/98	14500	314

Table 1.5 Data for the Employees table

11 Make the fields wider if necessary so that all the entries are shown in full.

12 Print preview the table. Use the Toolbar button.

13 Change to landscape orientation. **Remember**: File, Page setup.

14 Print the table. Use the Toolbar button.

15 Close down the table. **Remember**: File, Close.

16 Close down Access. **Remember**: File, Exit.

→ Practise your skills 2: Holidays

You are asked to create a database for a travel agent to hold information about holidays. Look back at the methods for each task if you need to.

Instructions:

1 Start up the computer.

2 Start up Microsoft Access.

3 Choose to create a blank Access database.

4 Save your new database file in your Access Databases folder. Give the file the name **Holidays**.

5 Create a table in Design view.

6 Set up the table structure as shown. There is no need to enter a description. Remember that the field size or format needs to be set in the Field Properties section in the lower part of the Table design window. Do not type the field size in the description column.

Field name	Data type	Field size or format
Resort	Text	25
Country	Text	20
StartDate	Date/Time	Short Date
Days	Number	Long Integer
Price	Currency	2 decimal places
Deposit	Currency	2 decimal places

Table 1.6 Structure of the Holidays table

7 Save the table structure. Give the table the name **Holidays Table**. Add your name in brackets to the table name.

8 Do not allow Access to create a primary key.

9 Change to Datasheet view.

10 Enter records as shown:

Resort	Country	Start date	Days	Price	Deposit
Lake Como	Italy	02/06/02	7	£415.00	£100.00
Cortina	Italy	25/07/02	10	£775.00	£200.00
Torbole	Italy	25/07/02	14	£765.00	£200.00
Wengen	Switzerland	26/07/02	7	£439.00	£100.00
Interlaken	Switzerland	14/06/02	7	£545.00	£150.00
Zermatt	Switzerland	19/07/02	7	£535.00	£150.00
Kaprun	Austria	08/08/02	14	£649.00	£175.00
St Johann	Austria	14/06/02	7	£425.00	£100.00
Alpbach	Austria	25/07/02	10	£530.00	£150.00

Table 1.7 Data for the Holidays table

11 Make the fields wider if necessary so that all the entries are shown in full.

12 Print preview the table.

13 Change to landscape orientation.

14 Print the table.

15 Close down the table.

16 Close down Access.

→ Check your knowledge

1 One row of a database table, holding data about one person or item, is called a...

2 Each row of the table is divided into columns called...

3 At the top of each column is a heading called the...

4 When you save a database on a computer, it is stored as a...

5 What is another name for a folder?

6 Which of the following data items must be stored in a text field? (More than one answer)

   a SO12 6GH

   b 12/05/02

   c (01998)345678

   d 397.59

   e 4563823a

7 Name two types of number field that would be suitable for storing whole numbers.

8 Name two types of number field that would be suitable for storing numbers that have a fractional (decimal) part, such as 23.45 or 109.5.

9 What field type would you use to store sums of money such as £25.50, if you want to display the pound sign?

10 What field type would you use to store 15/11/02?

You will learn to

- Identify and access existing data files/tables
- For a given database, identify the structure in terms of field names and data types
- Open an existing database and display the records and fields for editing
- Add new data to a record
- Add a new record to an existing database
- Edit data
- Delete a record
- Sort the records in a table/file in ascending or descending order (a) alphabetical (b) numeric
- Save the modified database
- Print a sorted list of all the records in a table/file including all the fields

Task 2.1 — Identify and access existing data files/tables

You will open the training database that you created in Section 1.

Method

1 Start up the computer system if it is not already running. Start up Microsoft Access from the Start button.
2 The Microsoft Access opening task pane should appear on the right of the Access window.

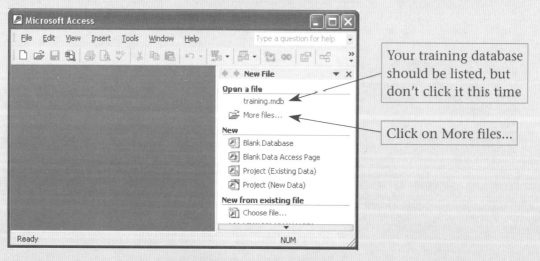

Your training database should be listed, but don't click it this time

Click on More files...

Figure 2.1 The Microsoft Access opening window with task pane

3 Look at the Open a file section. Your training database should be listed.

4 Click on More Files . . .

5 The Open dialogue box appears. Double click on your Access Databases folder to open it.

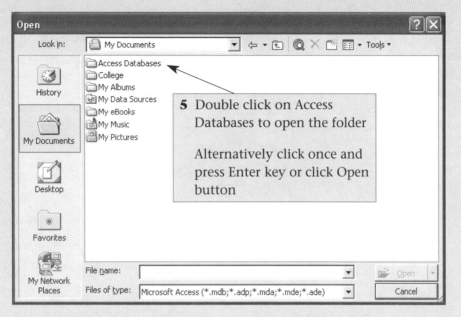

Figure 2.2 The Open dialogue box

6 Your database files should now be listed. Double click on the name of your training database file to open it.

Remember:

If the double click is difficult for you, there is an alternative. Click once then press the Enter key on the keyboard.

Note:

Your training database is probably on the list of recently opened files. Normally you would select it and click OK to open it. You are not doing so this time, because you need to learn how to find and open files that are not on the list, as well as those that are on the list.

Task 2.2	For a given database, identify the structure in terms of field names and data types

Your training database file should open. Its database window should be displayed inside the Access window, with its name, training: Database, shown in the title bar. The Tables button should appear to be pushed in. The name of your table, Training Courses (Your Name), should be displayed.

You know the structure of this table, because you created it yourself. You may be asked later to write down the structure of a table that you have not seen before. The following method takes you through the stages of identifying a table structure.

Method

1 Click on the name of the table if it is not already selected.
2 Click the Design button to open the table in Design view.

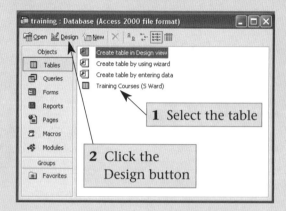

Figure 2.3 The training: Database window showing tables

3 You should now see the design window listing the field names and field types.
4 Take a sheet of paper. Write the name of the table at the top and draw three columns. Give the columns headings: Field name, Data type, and Field size/format.

Field name	Data type	Field size/format

Table 2.1 Writing down the table structure

5 Copy the list of field names and data types from the design window to your sheet of paper.
6 Click on each field name in turn so that its field properties show in the lower part of the window. Write down the field size or format of each field in the third column on your paper.
7 You have now written down the structure of the table. You can check it against the original structure of the table as given in Section 1 Table 1.2, in the information before Task 1.7. You would be able to write down the structure in the same way for a table that you had not seen before.

Task 2.3   Open an existing database and display the records and fields for editing

Method

1 As you already have the table open in Design view, you can click the View button on the toolbar to switch to Datasheet view.
2 Look at the table. Make sure that you can identify the records (one row for each course), the fields and the field names.

| Task 2.4 | Add an extra field to a table |

The training company has decided that the database should include the maximum number of places available on each course. This will involve adding an extra field to the table.

Method

1	Switch to Design view of the table.
2	Add a new field name, **Places**, below Course Code.
3	Change the data type to Number.
4	The description should be **Maximum places available**.
5	In the Field Properties section, keep Long Integer as the field size.
6	Click the Save icon on the toolbar to save the altered table structure.

| Task 2.5 | Add new data to a record |

Method

1 Switch to Datasheet view of the table.
2 Enter data into the new Places field of each record:

Course Name	Location	Date	Price	Sessions	Course code	Places
Introducing your PC	Liverpool	14/10/02	£250.00	2	287a	20
Introducing your PC	Bristol	19/10/02	£250.00	2	287b	20
Introducing your PC	London	28/10/02	£250.00	2	287c	20
Introducing the Internet	Liverpool	15/10/02	£250.00	2	288a	20
Introducing the Internet	Liverpool	24/10/02	£250.00	2	288b	20
Networking Essentials	London	27/10/02	£625.75	3	417a	15
Website Development	London	20/10/02	£300.00	1	501a	20
PC Troubleshooting	London	12/10/02	£425.50	2	704a	15
PC Troubleshooting	Liverpool	23/10/02	£425.50	2	704b	15
Upgrading a PC	London	18/10/02	£600.00	3	705a	15

Table 2.2 Data for the new Places field

Hint:

It is best to get the design right first time and include all the fields that will be needed. Unfortunately this is not always possible. Requirements for the database may change after it has been in use for a while. It is easy to add a field to the table structure. The time-consuming task comes afterwards if you then have to enter data into the new field for many existing records.

Method

1   Look at the row just below the last record. There should be an asterisk (*) in the left margin. This means that the row is available for entering a new record.

	PC Troubleshooting	Liverpool	23/10/2002
	Upgrading a PC	London	18/10/2002
*			

Figure 2.4 Row available for a new record

2   Click into the first column of this row. As you click, the asterisk should be replaced by a black triangle. This means that the row is selected.

	PC Troubleshooting	Liverpool	23/10/2002
	Upgrading a PC	London	18/10/2002
▶			

Figure 2.5 Row selected

3   Start to key in the word **Upgrading**. The black triangle should be replaced with a picture of a pencil. This means that the record is being edited and that the current changes have not yet been saved. At the same time, a new row appears below the record you are editing.

	PC Troubleshooting	Liverpool	23/10/2002
	Upgrading a PC	London	18/10/2002
✎	Up		
*			

Figure 2.6 Row being edited

4   Continue entering data into the record as follows:

Upgrading a PC	Liverpool	29/10/02	£600.00	3	705b	15

Table 2.3 Data for a new record

5   Press the Tab key to move down to the next row. As you leave the record you have just keyed in, the pencil disappears and the record is automatically saved.

6   Enter two more records:

PC Troubleshooting	Bristol	30/10/02	£425.50	2	704c	15
Introducing the Internet	London	31/10/02	£250.00	2	288c	20

Table 2.4 Data for two new records

7   Tab or click out of this last record into any other record so that the last record is saved.

Task 2.7 Edit data

The website development course is to be held in London instead of Bristol, and the fee is being reduced to £300. Alter the record.

Method

I	Find the record for Website Development, Course Code 501a. Click into its Location field, delete **Bristol** and key in **London**.
2	Delete the price of **£350.25** and enter the new price of **£300**.
3	Tab or click out of the record so that it is saved.

Task 2.8 Delete a record

The training course on PC Troubleshooting in London on 12/10/02 has to be cancelled. Delete the record from the table.

Hint:

If you are not confident that you are deleting the right record, click No and the record will not be deleted. You can then check and try again.

Method

I	Click into any field in the record you want to delete. The black triangle should appear in the left margin to show that the record is selected.
2	Click the Delete Record button on the toolbar ▶✗
3	A warning message appears, asking if you are sure you want to delete the record. Click Yes to confirm that you want to delete.

Task 2.9 Sort the records in a table alphabetically in ascending or descending order

Hint:

The 'new' record at the bottom of the table, marked by the asterisk, is not included in the sorting. It stays at the bottom. Any other empty records will be included in the sort and will move to the top of the table. If you have accidentally introduced extra empty records then delete them.

Sort the courses by location, first ascending (A to Z) then descending (Z to A).

Method

I	Click in the Location field of any record.
2	Click on the Sort Ascending button on the toolbar ⬆
3	Check to see that the records are sorted alphabetically in ascending order of location.
4	Click on the Sort Decending button on the toolbar ⬇
5	Check to see that the records are sorted alphabetically in descending order of location.

Task 2.10 — Sort the records in a table numerically in ascending or descending order

Sort the records in order of the course price, first ascending then descending.

Method

I	Click in the Price field of any record.
2	Click on the Sort Ascending button on the toolbar $\frac{A}{Z}\downarrow$
3	Check to see that the records are sorted in ascending order of price.
4	Click on the Sort Decending button on the toolbar $\frac{Z}{A}\downarrow$
5	Check to see that the records are sorted in descending order of price.

Information: Alphabetical and numerical sorting

Suppose that you have saved the following numbers in a field with the Number data type.

189, 84, 27, 602, 13, 8

You sort in ascending order. The numbers are sorted according to their values.

8, 13, 27, 84, 189, 602

Suppose that you saved the same numbers in a text field. Perhaps they are catalogue numbers that will not be needed for any calculations. You sort in ascending order. This is a text field, so its contents will be sorted alphabetically, starting with the first character. The result will be:

13, 189, 27, 602, 8, 84

The first character of 189 is 1. 1 is smaller than the first character of 27, which is 2. 189 therefore comes before 27, even though 189 is bigger than 27 as a number.

Number digits come before letters in alphabetical sorts. Spaces come before number digits. Here are the names of some firms, sorted alphabetically.

0 0 A to B Taxis (notice the spaces)
000-999 Abba Emergency Services
3D Aluminium Double Glazing
4 Most Driving School
A 1 Motors
ABC Taxis

You may accidentally key in a space at the start of a data entry, and not notice that it is there. When you sort alphabetically, the space will take the entry to the top of the list, giving an unexpected result. Check for unwanted spaces if one of your records seems to be sorted into the wrong position.

Task 2.11   Save the modified database

If you make any changes to the structure of a table then you must save those changes before you close the table. Changes to the contents of records are saved automatically when you move out of the record. Sorting a table changes its structure, so the table needs to be saved.

Method

1   Click the Save icon on the toolbar.

Task 2.12   Print a sorted list of all the records in a table/file, including all the fields

To print a sorted list of records, you simply sort the table then print it.

Method

1   Check that the table is still sorted in descending order of price.
2   Click the Print Preview button.
3   Inspect the Print Preview window. Probably the display is in portrait orientation, and there are two pages because the table is too wide to fit on one page.
4   Change to landscape orientation. The table should now fit on one page.
5   Print the table.

Remember:

To change orientation, click File and select Page Setup from the drop down list. Click on the Page tab and select the orientation.

Task 2.13   Print a selected record from a table

Print out the record for the course on Website Development only.

Method

1   If you are still looking at the Print Preview window, click the button labelled Close on the toolbar. This will return you to Datasheet view of the table.
2   Click in the margin next to the record for the course on Website Development. You click in the grey area where the triangle appears when the record is selected. The whole row should be highlighted in a changed colour.
3   Click on the File menu to open the drop down list. Select Print. (Do not use the Print icon on the toolbar.)

4   The Print dialogue box appears.
5   Click on the Option button labelled Selected Records.
6   Click OK.

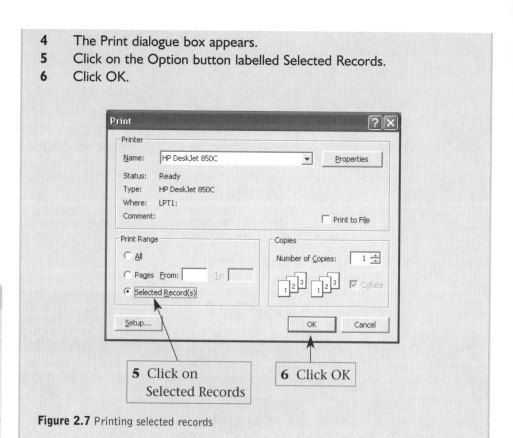

Hint:

This is one of the few times when you do not print preview before you print. Change to landscape orientation if necessary before you go to the Print dialogue box.

5 Click on Selected Records

6 Click OK

Figure 2.7 Printing selected records

Remember:

Are you taking regular breaks away from the computer?

Task 2.14   Close down

Close the table.
Close down Access.

→ Practise your skills 1: Employees

You are asked to make some changes to the employees database. The instructions will include some reminders, but the methods will not be given in detail. Look back at the detailed methods for each task if you need to.

Instructions:

1 Start up Microsoft Access.

2 Open your employees database file. You can select it from the recently used files list if it is there.

3 Open your Employees table in Design view. Use the Design button.

4 Inspect the Design view and write down the structure of the table in three columns headed Field name, Data type and Field size/format. Check your structure against the original structure that was given in Section 1, Practise your skills 1.

5 Still in Design view, add an extra field to the table. Call it BirthDate. Give it the Date/Time data type and format to Short Date.

6 Save the table structure.

7 Switch to Datasheet view of the table.

8 Enter data in the new field as in Table 2.5:

Payroll No	BirthDate
302	02/06/72
303	08/10/71
304	06/07/68
305	21/08/62
309	19/02/69
307	28/01/70
308	30/06/59
306	22/08/63
310	25/11/74
311	31/05/63
312	04/10/52
313	14/08/82
314	30/09/58

Table 2.5 Data for BirthDate field

9 Add two more records:

Surname	Initials	Title	Branch	StartDate	Salary	Payroll No	BirthDate
Lee	C	Cashier	Leeds	02/09/02	11500	315	23/09/80
Smith	M	Cashier	Reading	02/09/02	11500	316	05/08/81

Table 2.6 Two new records for the Employees table

10 M B Adams of Leeds has had a pay rise to 12000. Edit the record to change the Salary amount.

11 K Erikson of Reading has moved to the Newbury branch. Edit the record to show this change.

12 H Ford has left. Delete the record. **Hint**: Click into the record and use the Delete button on the toolbar.

13 Sort the records in ascending order of start date. **Hint**: Click into the StartDate field and use the Toolbar button.

14 Save the altered table structure.

15 Print preview, then print out all the records on one sheet of paper. Use landscape orientation.

16 Close the table and close the database.

→ Practise your skills 2: Holidays

You are asked to make some changes to the holidays database. Look back at the detailed methods for each task if you need to.

Instructions:

1 Start up Microsoft Access.

2 Open your holidays database file. You can select it from the recently used files list if it is there.

3 Open your Holidays table in Design view.

4 Inspect the Design view and write down the structure of the table in three columns headed Field name, Data type and Field size/format. Check your structure against the original structure that was given in Section 1, Practise your skills 2.

5 Still in Design view, add an extra field to the table. Call it Airport. Give it the Text data type and a field size of 20.

6 Save the table structure.

7 Switch to Datasheet view of the table.

8 Enter data in the new field as follows:

Resort	Airport
Lake Como	Milan
Cortina	Milan
Torbole	Milan
Wengen	Zurich
Interlaken	Geneva
Zermatt	Zurich
Kaprun	Salzburg
St Johann	Salzburg
Alpbach	Innsbruck

Table 2.7 Data for the Airport field

9 Add three more records:

Resort	Country	Start date	Days	Price	Deposit	Airport
Lake Constance	Germany	17/08/02	14	£1,166.00	£200.00	Zurich
Lake Geneva	Switzerland	17/08/02	7	£519.00	£120.00	Geneva
Seefeld	Austria	10/08/02	14	£820.00	£200.00	Innsbruck

Table 2.8 Three new records for the Holidays table

10 The price of the holiday in Cortina has been reduced to £750. Edit the record to change the price.

11 The airport for the holiday in Interlaken has been changed from Geneva to Zurich. Edit the record to show this change.

12 The holiday in Torbole is cancelled. Delete the record.

13 Sort the records in ascending order of price.

14 Save the altered table structure.

15 Print preview, then print out all the records on one sheet of paper. Use landscape orientation.

16 Close the table and close the database.

→ Check your knowledge

In questions 1, 2 and 3, imagine that you are looking at a database table in Datasheet view.

1   One of the records has a black triangle next to it in the left margin. What does the black triangle mean?

2   One of the records has a picture of a pencil next to it in the left margin. What does the pencil mean?

3   The bottom row is empty and has an asterisk (*) next to it in the left margin. What does the asterisk mean?

4   You add a new field to an existing table. Must you save the table now?

5   You edit a record in a table by changing a salary from £14500 to £14600. Must you save the table now?

6   One of the fields in a table is too narrow to display all the data, so you make the field wider. Must you save the table?

7   The following numbers are saved in a field with the Number data type, and sorted in ascending order. Write down the numbers in their sorted order: 62, 700, 130, 22, 7.

8   The same numbers are saved in a field with the Text data type and sorted in ascending order. Write down the numbers in their sorted order.

9   The surnames Varju, Adkins, Wilkins and Smith are stored in a text field and sorted in ascending order. They appear in the order Smith, Adkins, Varju, Wilkins. Suggest a likely cause for this problem with sorting.

10 You print preview a database table and find that one of the fields is on a second page. What might you do to print the database table on one sheet of paper?

You are asked to create and maintain a database to record sales of computers. You may need to look back at the tasks in Sections 1 and 2 to see the details of the methods.

Instructions:

Hint:

When you see the File New Database window, find and click the yellow Create New Folder button on the toolbar. This lets you create a new folder.

1 Create a new directory (folder) inside your Access Databases folder. Call your new directory **Sales**. (See Tasks 1.3 and 1.4 of Section 1.)

2 Create a new Access database called Computers.mdb and save it in your Sales directory.

3 Create a new table in your Computers.mdb database and give it the following structure:

Field name	Data type	Field size or format
Model	Text	20
Processor (MHz)	Number	Long Integer
Memory (MB)	Number	Long Integer
Price	Currency	2 decimal places
Sale date	Date/Time	Medium Date
Printer included	Text	1

Table 2.9 Structure of the Computers table

4 Save your table with the name Computers, and add your name in brackets to the table name.

5 Switch to Datasheet view of the table and enter data as follows:

Model	Processor (MHz)	Memory (MB)	Price	Sale date	Printer
Advent 3979 BTO	1800	256	£939.20	10-Jun-02	N
CCL Home KP	1800	256	£939.50	28-May-02	N
Holly KA 1.7	1700	256	£988.99	08-Jun-02	Y
Net a2000 Pro	2000	256	£990.00	09-Jun-02	Y
eMachines 130 CD	900	128	£449.00	10-Jun-02	N
eMachines 540	1300	256	£699.99	11-Jun-02	N
NEC Powermate	1000	128	£569.99	06-Jun-02	Y
HP Vectra XE310	1000	128	£609.83	12-Jun-02	N
Advent 7003	2000	512	£1,799.00	08-Jun-02	N

Table 2.10 Data for the Computers table

6 Print the table on one sheet of paper, making sure that all entries are shown in full. Write **Printout 1** in pen on the printout.

7 The sale date for the NEC Powermate was entered wrongly. Correct it to 05-Jun-02.

8 The eMachines 540 was sold with a printer at a price of £904.50. Make the correction.

9 Add two more records.

Model	Processor (MHz)	Memory (MB)	Price	Sale date	Printer
Compaq Evo N160	933	128	£809.58	14-Jun-02	N
Tiny Home Plus 1000	1000	128	£599.00	14-Jun-02	N

Table 2.11 Two more records for the Computers table

10 Records for May are no longer required. Delete the record for the CCL Home KP.

11 Add an extra field with the name **Type**. It should be a text field with a field size of 10.

12 Enter data into the new field as follows:

Model	Type
Advent 3979 BTO	Desktop
Holly KA 1.7	Desktop
Net a2000 Pro	Desktop
eMachines 130 CD	Desktop
eMachines 540	Desktop
NEC Powermate	Desktop
HP Vectra XE310	Desktop
Advent 7003	Laptop
Compaq Evo N160	Laptop
Tiny Home Plus 1000	Desktop

Table 2.12 Data for the Type field

13 Delete the Memory (MB) field.

14 Sort the records in descending order of processor speed.

15 Print all the records in their sorted order on one sheet of paper. Write **Printout 2** in pen on the printout.

16 Sort the records in ascending order of Model.

17 Print all the records in their sorted order on one sheet of paper. Write **Printout 3** in pen on the printout.

18 Print out the record for the NEC Powermate only. Write **Printout 4** in pen on the printout.

19 Save any changes to the table design, then close the table.

20 Close down Access.

You will learn to

- Use a query to sort records
- Use a query to select records
- Print a list of all records in a table/file matched by a single condition search
- Print only selected fields from the records in a table/file
- Print a list of all records in a table/file matched by a single condition search, but including only selected fields from the records
- Identify relational operators
- Use relational operators in a query

Information: Database objects

Start Access and open your training database file.

The familiar database window is displayed on the screen. At the left of the window are buttons labelled Tables, Queries, Forms, Reports, Pages, Macros, Modules. These are all kinds of database **objects**. At Level 1 you use tables and queries, but here, for interest, is an outline of the purposes of all these objects.

- A **table** is a storage container for data. The data is organised into records and fields. You have created and used several tables, including the training courses table in this database file.

- A **query** is used to sort records into a chosen order, or to select chosen records for display. For example, you could select records of all courses held in Liverpool. A query does not store any data. It uses data from one or more tables. You will be using queries in this section.

- A **form** is used to display data on the screen, usually one record at a time. The form does not store any data. It uses data from a table. Forms are convenient for entering, viewing and editing records.

- A **report** is used to set out data on a page for printing. If you print a table, you have very little control over the layout and appearance of the printout. A report lets you take the data from a table and control how it appears on the page.

- A **page** is used to set out data for display as a web page on the Internet.

- **Macros** and **modules** are used to automate a database. Database designers can create complete applications to manage a database and control how people can use it.

A database can include many objects. Access saves all the objects belonging to a database in one file. There are other database applications that save each table, query etc. in a separate file.

In this section you will be using queries to display and print data from a table. You can display records sorted in different orders. You can select the records to be displayed. You can also choose which fields to display.

Task 3.1   Create a query

Method

1   Open your training database if it is not already open.
Click on the Queries button in the training: Database window.
2   The window displays two ways of creating a new query.
Double click on Create query in Design view.

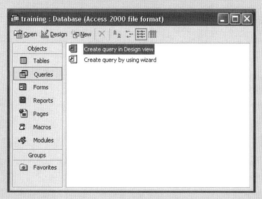

Figure 3.1 Queries section of the database window

3   The Query design window appears.
In front of it is the Show Table dialogue box.

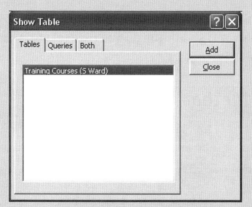

Figure 3.2 The Show Table dialogue box

4   There is only one table, so it is already selected. If there were several tables then you would need to select the table on which to base the query. Click Add.
5   Click Close to close the Show Table dialogue box.

6   Look at the Query design window. It has a title bar with a temporary name for the query: Query1. It is a Select query. This is the simplest form of query and it is used for selecting records for display.

7   The upper section of the window shows the table on which the query is based, with a list of the fields in the table.

8   The lower section of the window is where you specify what you want the query to do. This area is the Query design grid.

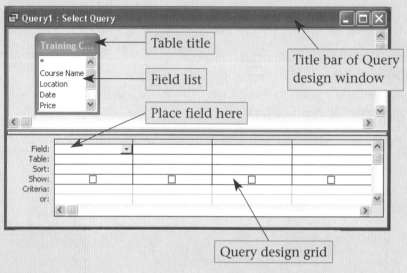

Figure 3.3 Query design window

Remember:

A query does not store data. It uses data from a table. Every time you create a query, you have to specify which table it should use.

Task 3.2   Add all fields to a query design

You will use all the fields from the table in this query. The method gives a quick way of adding all the fields. Later you will learn how to add fields one at a time.

Method

1   Double click on the table title in the upper section of the window. The list of fields should be selected, with a blue background.

2   Point the mouse to any field name in the list. Hold down the left mouse button and drag the mouse down to the lower part of the window, to the top left box in the Query design grid. The mouse pointer should change to look like a stack of three rectangles. Release the mouse button.

3   The field names from the table should be displayed in the top row of the Query design grid. The name of the table should appear in the second row.

4 Check that all the field names are in the grid. You may need to use the scroll bar to scroll to the right.

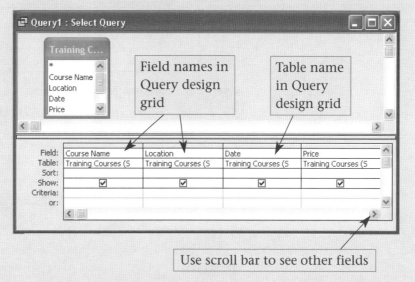

Field names in Query design grid

Table name in Query design grid

Use scroll bar to see other fields

Figure 3.4 Query design window with field names

Task 3.3 | Switch between Design and Datasheet view of a query

Method

1   Click the View button on the toolbar to switch to Datasheet view.
2   Click the View button to switch back to Design view.

Hint:

The Datasheet view of the query should look just like the Datasheet view of the table at the moment. You have not yet put in any instructions for the query to sort or select records.

Information: Sorting records by using a query

You have already sorted records in a table. Sorting in a table is quick and easy, but you cannot save the results of the sorting. When you do another sort, your old sort is lost. If you sort records using a query, you can save the query with the sorting instructions. You can then go back to the query any time you want to display or print the records in their sorted order.

Task 3.4 | Use a query to sort records

You will sort the records alphabetically by course name.

Method

1   The Query design window should be displayed on the screen.
2   The third row of the Query design grid is the sort row. Click into the first column of this row. This is the Course Name column.
3   An arrow appears. Click on it to show a drop down list.

4   Select Ascending from the list.

Field:	Course Name	Location
Table:	Training Courses (S	Training Courses (S
Sort:	Ascending	
Show:	☑	☑
Criteria:		
or:		

Set up sorting here

Figure 3.5 Sorting records with a query

5   Switch to Datasheet view and check that the records have been sorted alphabetically by course name.

6   Switch back to Design view.

Task 3.5   Save a query

Method

1   Click the Save icon on the toolbar.

2   A Save As box appears, asking for the query name.

3   Key in the name **qrySortName (your name)** and click OK. Put your own name in the brackets.

4   Check that the name has appeared in the title bar of the Query design window.

Hint:

Add your own name to query names, just as you added it to table names. Your name will then show when you print the query.

Information: Naming queries

There is a convention that query names should start with the three lower case letters qry. The rest of the name should describe the purpose of the query. It is a good idea to get in the habit of following the convention. You may eventually create large databases with many objects, and write code to control the objects. It then becomes important that you can easily recognise which objects are queries. The qry naming convention helps with this.

You would not normally add your own name to a query name. You need to do it while working on this unit so that your name appears on your printouts.

Task 3.6   Print a query

Method

1   Switch to Datasheet view.

2   Click the Print Preview button on the toolbar.

3   Check the preview. Probably some of the fields are on a second page.

4   Change to landscape orientation, just as you did with tables.

5   Click the Print icon to print the results of the query.

6   Close the query by clicking on the File menu and choosing Close.

Hint:

Access will not 'remember' that the query was printed in landscape orientation. If you open the query and want to print it again, you will need to set landscape orientation again.

Task 3.7 — Use a query to select records by text

You will make a new query to display only the training courses held in Liverpool.

Method

1 Start with the database window. The queries section of the window should be showing.
2 Double click on Create query in Design view.
3 The Show Table dialogue box shows, with the table selected. Click Add, then click Close.
4 Double click on the table name to select all the fields in the list.
5 Drag the fields to the Query design grid as you did for the previous query.
6 The fifth row of the grid is labelled Criteria. This is where you enter the information needed for selecting records. Click into the Criteria row in the Location column.
7 Key in **Liverpool** and press the Enter key.
8 Double quote marks should appear round the word Liverpool.

Figure 3.6 Selecting courses in Liverpool

9 Switch to Datasheet view. You should see the records for courses in Liverpool.
10 Check that all the correct records are shown. It is useful if you have a printout of the complete table to help you check the query results.
11 Save the query with the name **qryLiverpool(your name)**.
12 Preview the query, change to landscape orientation and print.
13 Close the query.

Information: Criteria using text

When you key in a piece of text, such as Liverpool, in the Criteria row of a field, Access will search that field of the table, trying to find exactly the text you keyed in. It searches for Liverpool. When it finds Liverpool in the Location field of a record, it selects the record. You must be careful to key in exactly the text that can be found in the field. If you make a spelling mistake such as Livrepool in the Criteria row then Access will not select the records containing Liverpool. It is also important that there are no spelling mistakes in the table itself.

The word 'criteria' is plural. You will also meet the singular form, 'criterion'.

Open and modify a query

You will open your Liverpool query again and sort the records by price, in ascending order.

Method

1 The database window should be open with the queries section displayed.
2 Click on the name of your qryLiverpool query to select it.
3 Click the Design button in the database window. This opens the query in Design view.
4 Click in the Sort row in the Price column so that an arrow appears.
5 Click the arrow and select Ascending from the drop down list.

Field:	Course Name	Location	Date	Price
Table:	Training Courses (S	Training Courses (S	Training Courses (S	Training Courses (S
Sort:				Ascending
Show:	☑	☑	☑	☑
Criteria:		"Liverpool"		
or:				

Figure 3.7 Sort by Price, ascending

6 Switch to Datasheet view and check that the Liverpool courses are sorted in order of price, lowest price first.
7 Click the Save button on the toolbar to save the query. You will not be asked for a name again. The new version of the query will replace the old version, keeping the same name.
8 Close the query. There is no need to print it.

Task 3.9 — Use a query to select records by a number

You will create a query to display the records for courses that have 2 sessions.

Method

1 Start with the database window. The queries section of the window should be showing.
2 Double click on Create query in Design view.
3 The Show Table dialogue box shows, with the table selected. Click Add, then click Close.
4 Double click on the table name to select all the fields in the list.
5 Drag the fields to the Query design grid.
6 Click into the Criteria row in the Sessions column.
7 Key in **2** and press the Enter key.
8 Notice that no quote marks appear round the number 2.

Field:	Course Name	Location	Date	Price	Sessions
Table:	Training Courses (S	Training Courses (S	Training Courses (S	Training Courses (S	Training Courses (S
Sort:					
Show:	☑	☑	☑	☑	☑
Criteria:					2
or:					

Figure 3.8 Selecting courses with 2 sessions

9   Switch to Datasheet view. You should see 8 records, all for courses with 2 sessions. If you have a printout of the whole table, check that your query has selected all the right records.

10   Click the Save button, and save your query with the name qry2sessions.

11   Close the query. There is no need to print it.

Task 3.10   Use a query to select records by date

You will create a query to display the record for any course held on 27/10/02.

Method

1   Start with the database window. The queries section of the window should be showing.

2   Double click on Create query in Design view.

3   The Show Table dialogue box shows, with the table selected. Click Add, then click Close.

4   Double click on the table name to select all the fields in the list.

5   Drag the fields to the Query design grid.

6   Click into the Criteria row in the Date column.

7   Key in **27/10/02** and press the Enter key.

8   Hash marks (#) should appear round the date. They show that Access has recognised your entry as a date. If you see quote marks instead, then delete the whole entry and try again.

Field:	Course Name	Location	Date
Table:	Training Courses (S	Training Courses (S	Training Courses (S
Sort:			
Show:	☑	☑	☑
Criteria:			#27/10/2002#
or:			

Figure 3.9 Selecting courses on 27/10/02

9   Switch to Datasheet view. There should be one record, the Networking Essentials course.

10   Click the Save button, and save your query with the name qry27Oct.

11   Close the query. There is no need to print it.

Remember:

Take regular breaks. You could close the database and close Access at this stage, then open the database when you start again.

Information: Criteria and data types

Access needs to distinguish between text, numbers and dates when they are used in the criteria row of a Query design grid. You have seen that it will put double quotes round text and put hash marks round dates but leave ordinary numbers alone. Criteria need to have a data type that matches the data type of their field. If you key in text as a criterion in a date field or key in a date as a criterion in a number field then you will see an error message when you press the Enter key.

So far you have included all the fields from the table in your queries. Next you will use a query to print out only the Course Name, Location and Date fields for all records. You will do this using two different methods. In Method 1 you will put in all the fields but hide the ones that are not to be shown. In Method 2 you will put in only the fields that are to be shown.

Method 1

1 Start with the database window. The queries section of the window should be showing.
2 Double click on Create query in Design view.
3 The Show Table dialogue box shows, with the table selected. Click Add, then click Close.
4 Double click on the table name to select all the fields in the list.
5 Drag the fields to the Query design grid.
6 The fourth row of the Query design grid is labelled 'Show'. Each field has a square check box with a tick in it. This tick means that the field will show in the query results.
7 Leave the ticks in the boxes in the Course Name, Location and Date fields. Click in the boxes in the other fields to remove the ticks. You may need to scroll sideways to see the fields at the right-hand end of the grid.

Field:	Course Name	Location	Date	Price	Sessions	Course Code
Table:	Training Courses (S	Training Courses (S	Training Courses (S	Training Courses (S	Training Courses (S	Training Courses (S
Sort:						
Show:	☑	☑	☑	☐	☐	☐
Criteria:						
or:						

Figure 3.10 Hiding fields in a query

8 Change to Datasheet view. You should see only three fields: Course Name, Location and Date.
9 Save the query with the name qryCourseLocationDate.
10 Print preview the query. Check the display, then print the query.
11 Close the query.

Method 2

1 Start with the database window. The queries section of the window should be showing.
2 Double click on Create query in Design view.
3 The Show Table dialogue box shows, with the table selected. Click Add, then click Close.
4 Do **not** put in the fields as you have done before. Instead click on the arrow in the top left box of the Query design grid. A drop down list should appear.

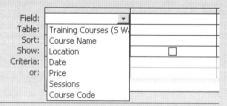

Figure 3.11 Putting one field into a Query design grid

5   Click on Course Name to select it from the list. The Course Name field goes into the first column of the grid.
6   Click into the first row of the second column so that an arrow appears. Click on the arrow to show the drop down list.
7   Select Location from the drop down list. The Location field goes into the second column of the grid.
8   Put the Date field into the third column of the grid in the same way.
9   Switch to Datasheet view. The three fields should be displayed.
10 Close the query. There is no need to save or print it.

Information: Other ways of placing fields

You have learned two ways of putting fields into the Query design grid. You might like to try out two others.

1   In the top part of the Query design window, point the mouse to one of the field names. Hold down the left mouse button as you drag the field name down to one of the columns of the Query design grid.
2   In the top part of the Query design window, double click on one of the field names. The field name will appear in the first empty column of the Query design grid.

It does not matter which method you use. Choose the method that you prefer.

| Task 3.12 | Print a list of all records in a table/ file matched by a single condition search, but including only selected fields from the records |

You will use a query to print out the course names and dates for courses held in London. You will use a combination of methods that you have already learned.

Method

1   Create a new query in Design view and add the table so that the list of fields shows in the top part of the Query design window.
2   Put the Course Name, Location and Date fields into the Query design grid. You can do this using the drop down list, or by one of the methods given in the information above.
3   In the Criteria row of the Location field, key in **London**.
4   Switch to Datasheet view and check that all the records for London courses are shown, and no others.
5   Switch back to Design view.

Hint:

You have to include the Location field in the query so that you can use it to select the London courses. You were not asked to show the location, so it is important that you remember to hide the Location field before printing the query. It is worth checking that the selection is correct while the Location field is still showing, because it is easier to check that you have the right records.

Hint:

You could close the database and take a break here.

6   You were asked to print out the course names and dates, but you were not asked to print out the location, so click in the check box in the Show row of the Location field to remove the tick.

Field:	Course Name	Location	Date
Table:	Training Courses (S	Training Courses (S	Training Courses (S
Sort:			
Show:	☑	☐	☑
Criteria:		"London"	
or:			

Figure 3.12 London courses showing course name and date

7   Switch to Datasheet view again to check that you have only the Course Name and Date fields showing.
8   Save the query with the name qryLondonCourseDates(your name).
9   Preview and print the query.
10 Close the query.

Information: Relational operators

You have used queries to select records that have field contents which exactly match the criteria you keyed in. You found courses with exactly 2 sessions, and courses that are held on the exact date of 27/10/02. It is also possible to select courses with more than 2 sessions, or courses held before 27/10/02 and so on. To do this, you need to use **relational operators**.

The relational operators are:
= equals
> is greater than
< is less than
>= is greater than or equal to
<= is less than or equal to
<> is not equal to

Task 3.13   Use relational operators in a query to search by number

You will create a query to select records of courses with more than 2 sessions. You will need to use the operator > (is greater than). You will then change the query to show courses with 2 or more sessions, using the operator >= (is greater than or equal to). You will then change the query again to show courses that do not have 2 sessions, using the operator <> (is not equal to).

Method

1   Start with the query section of the training: Database window, and create a new query in Design view.
2   Add the table so that it appears in the top section of the window.
3   Put all the fields in the Query design grid, using any method.

4   In the criteria row of the Sessions field, key in >**2**.

Field:	Course Name	Location	Date	Price	Sessions	
Table:	Training Courses (S	Training Courses (S	Training Courses (S	Training Courses (S	Training Courses (S	
Sort:						
Show:	☑	☑	☑	☑	☑	
Criteria:					>2	
or:						

Figure 3.13 Selecting courses with more than 2 sessions

5   Switch to Datasheet view and check that it shows the records for courses with more than 2 sessions.
6   Switch back to Design view.
7   Sort the records in ascending order by Price.
8   Switch to Datasheet view to check the results of the combined selection and sorting.
9   Switch back to Design view.
10 Alter the criterion >**2** to >=**2** by adding the = sign.
11 Switch to Datasheet view. You should see the records for courses with 2 or more sessions.
12 Switch back to Design view.
13 Alter the criterion to <>**2**.
14 Switch to Datasheet view. You should see the records for all the courses that do not have 2 sessions. They have 1 or 3 sessions.
15 Close the query. You need not save or print it.

Task 3.14   Use relational operators in a query to search by currency

You will create a query to select records of courses costing less than £425.50. You will then change the query to select records of courses costing £425.50 or less.

Method

1   Create a new query in Design view and add the Training Courses table.
2   Put all the fields in the Query design grid.
3   In the Criteria row of the Price field, key in <**425.50**. (Do not key in the £ sign.) Press Enter.
4   Switch to Datasheet view. You should see the 7 records for courses costing less than £425.50.
5   Switch back to Design view.
6   Change the criterion <**425.50** to <=**425.50** by adding the = sign.
7   Switch to Datasheet view. You should see the records that you saw last time, but there should be two additional records for courses costing £425.50.
8   Close the query. You need not save or print it.

Task 3.15 — Use relational operators in a query to search by date

You will create a query to select records of courses held before 20/10/02. You will then change the query to select records of courses held on or before 20/10/02. Dates are stored as numbers. The later the date, the bigger the number. You can therefore use < (less than) to mean before, and > (greater than) to mean after.

Method

1. Create a new query in Design view and add the Training Courses table.
2. Put all the fields in the Query design grid.
3. In the Criteria row of the Date field, key in <**20/10/02**. Press Enter. Hash marks should appear round the date.
4. Switch to Datasheet view. You should see the 4 records for courses held before 20/10/02.
5. Switch back to Design view.
6. Change the criterion <**#20/10/02#** to <=**#20/10/02#** by adding the = sign.
7. Switch to Datasheet view. You should see the records that you saw last time, but there should be an additional record for the course on 20/10/02.
8. Switch back to Design view and sort the records in ascending order by date.
9. Switch to Datasheet view and check the result.
10. Close the query. You need not save or print it.

Task 3.16 — Using relational operators, execute searches on fields: text/character

You will create a query to select records of courses with names that come alphabetically after the letter M. You can use the relational operators with text. The criterion <M will select text that comes before M in alphabetical order. The criterion >M will select text that comes after M in alphabetical order.

Method

1. Create a new query in Design view and add the Training Courses table.
2. Put all the fields in the Query design grid.
3. In the Criteria row of the Course Name field, key in >**M**. Press Enter. Double quote marks should appear round the M.
4. Switch to Datasheet view. You should see the 6 records for courses with names that come alphabetically after M.
5. Switch back to Design view.
6. Change the criterion >**"M"** to <**"M"** by changing the sign.
7. Switch to Datasheet view. You should see the other 6 records: the ones with names that come alphabetically before M.

8 Switch back to Design view and sort these records by Course Name, ascending.

9 Switch to Datasheet view and check the result.

10 Close the query. You need not save or print it.

11 Close down the training database and close Access.

Information: Sorting out problems with select queries

Perhaps your query has not produced the results you expected. Perhaps you get an error message when you try to switch to Datasheet view. Here are some things to check.

- Did you key in your criterion in the correct column of the Criteria row? If you put London in the Course Name column then no matching records will be found. London has to go in the Location column.

- Did you key in exactly the text you are searching for? If you key in 'Introducing **the** PC' in the Course Name column then no matching records will be found. If you key in 'Introducing **your** PC' then records will be found.

- Did you key in dates in a format that Access can recognise? You can key in 20/10/02 or 20-Oct-02 and Access will recognise that this is a date. If you key in 20.10.02 then this will not be recognised as a date. It may be 'corrected' to 20:10:02 and treated as a time of day.

- Do not key in pound signs or commas when keying in currency or numbers. If you are searching for £25,000 then you should key in 25000. Check that no quote marks appear when you press the Enter key.

- If you are using a relational operator, did you choose the right one, and did you get the >= or <= sign the right way round? Keying in => or =< will not work.

- Always check your result with a full and up-to-date printout of the table. If a record is missing from the table then the query will not be able to find it.

→ Practise your skills 1: Employees

You are asked to create some queries based on your Employees table. Look back at the tasks earlier in this section if you are not sure of the methods. There is no need to print or save all the queries. You will be asked to save and print just a few of the queries for practice. Check all the results yourself and then compare them with the solutions at the end of the book.

Instructions:

1 Start Access and open your employees database.

2 Open your Employees table in Datasheet view, if you wish, to remind yourself of the contents.

3 Close the table.

4 Create a query to display all the records, sorted in ascending order of surname.

5 Save the query with the name qrySortSurname(your name).

6 Print out the query on one sheet of paper in landscape orientation. As this printout includes all the fields and all the records, you can use it instead of a table printout to help you check your other queries.

7 Create a query to select the records of cashiers, sorted in descending order of salary. Display the Surname, Initials, Branch and Salary fields only. **Hint**: You will need to include the Title field in the query, but hide it.

8 Save the query as qryCashiers(your name) and print it.

9 Create a query to select the records of employees whose salary is 11500. Sort the records in ascending order of birth date. Show all the fields.

10 Create a query to select the records of employees who started before 01/01/00. Sort in ascending order of starting date and show the Surname, Initials, Branch and StartDate fields.

11 Create a query to select the records of employees who earn £14500 or more. Sort the records alphabetically, ascending, by branch. Show the Surname, Initials, Branch and Salary fields.

12 Close all queries, close the database and close Access.

→ Practise your skills 2: Holidays

You are asked to create some queries based on your Holidays table. Look back at the tasks earlier in this section if you are not sure of the methods. There is no need to print or save all the queries. You will be asked to save and print just a few of the queries for practice. Check all the results yourself and then compare them with the solutions at the end of the book.

Instructions:

1 Start Access and open your holidays database.

2 Open your Holidays table in Datasheet view, if you wish, to remind yourself of the contents.

3 Close the table.

4 Create a query to display all the records, sorted in ascending order of resort.

5 Save the query with the name qrySortResort(your name).

6 Print out the query on one sheet of paper in landscape orientation. As this printout includes all the fields and all the records, you can use it instead of a table printout to help you check your other queries.

7 Create a query to select the holidays in resorts in Switzerland, sorted in ascending order of holiday price. Display the Resort, Startdate, Days and Price fields only. **Hint**: You will need to include the Country field in the query, but hide it.

8 Save the query as qrySwitzerland(your name) and print it.

9 Create a query to select the records of holidays lasting 7 days. Sort the records in ascending order of resort name. Show all the fields.

10 Create a query to select the records of holidays costing less than £600. Sort in ascending order of starting date and show the Resort, Country, Startdate and Airport fields.

11 Create a query to select the records of holidays starting on or after 25/07/02. Sort the records alphabetically, ascending, by airport. Show all the fields.

12 Close all queries, close the database and close Access.

→ Check your knowledge

1 Which database object is used for storing data?

2 Which database object is used for selecting chosen records for display?

3 You can sort records in a table or in a query. What is an advantage of sorting in a query?

In questions 4 to 10, imagine that you are creating a query based on the Holidays table. It has fields for Resort, Country, Startdate, Days, Price, Deposit and Airport. Try to answer without looking at the database.

4 You want to select holidays in Austria, so you key in **Austria** in the Criteria row of the Country field. What should appear round **Austria** when you press Enter or Tab?

5 You want to select holidays lasting for 7 days, so you key in **7** in the Criteria row of the Days field. What should appear round 7 when you press Enter or Tab?

6 You want to select holidays starting on 8th August 2002, so you key in **8/8/02** in the Criteria row of the Start date field. What should appear when you press Enter or Tab?

7 You want to select holidays lasting for 10 or more days. What should you put in the Criteria row, and which field should you put it in?

8 You want to select holidays in resorts with names that come alphabetically before S. What should you put in the Criteria row, and which field should you put it in?

9 You want to select holidays starting before 29th July 2002. What should you put in the Criteria row, and which field should you put it in?

10 You key in **17.08.02** in the Criteria row of the Start date field. How many records will be selected?

You will learn to

- Define database structure in terms of field names and data types
- Insert a new field
- Delete a field
- Change the field size

Task 4.1	Define the database structure in terms of field names and data types

When you created new database tables in Section 1, you were given the database structure. You had a list of field names, data types and field sizes or formats. In this section you will plan the database structure yourself, to suit a set of data.

Method

1 Look at the draft table of data. You are going to create a database to hold these and similar records of actors.

ACTOR NAME	EXPERIENCE	HEIGHT m	DATE OF BIRTH	FEE
Seymore Anya	Film	1.70	12/12/76	150
Clarke Chris	Film	1.85	02/07/81	100
Raven Damon	TV	1.80	05/09/78	120
Prince Paula	Stage	1.63	01/04/80	150
Carston Craig	TV	1.79	14/08/79	120
Bayliss Lauren	TV	1.68	25/04/81	120
Mayne Meriel	Film	1.66	28/02/79	100
Jackson Wayne	Stage	1.89	16/03/75	150

Table 4.1 Draft table of data for Actors database

2 On a sheet of paper, rule three columns and head them Field name, Data type and Field size/format.
3 In the first column, write down the field names as shown at the top of the draft table of data.

Field name	Data type	Field size/format
Actor name		
Experience		
Height m		
Date of Birth		
Fee		

Table 4.2 Starting the design of the Actors table

4   Actor name must be a text field. Write **Text** in the data type column opposite Actor name.
5   The field size must be big enough to hold any likely actor's name. Do not just think about the names given in the draft table of data. Think about any names that might possibly be added later. 40 characters should be enough, so write in **40** as the field size.
6   Experience must also be a **Text** field. Write that in.
7   Write in **20** characters as the field size. That should be enough.
8   The height in the table is given in metres to 2 decimal places. This has to be a number type, so write in **Number** as the data type.
9   You need a number type that will store numbers with decimal places. Single and Double are possibilities. Write in **Double 2 decimal places**, or Double 2dp.
10   Date of birth needs to be the **Date/Time** type, so write that in.
11   The dates are given in the short form, 12/12/76, rather than 12-Dec-76 or 12 December 1976. The format **Short Date** is needed, so write it in.
12   The fee is given as a whole number, without any £ sign. Write in the data type **Number**.
13   Another word for whole number is **integer**. You should choose one of the integer data types. The default type is **Long Integer**. Write it in.
14   Check your written design of the database structure. It should look like this.

Field name	Data type	Field size/format
Actor name	Text	40
Experience	Text	20
Height m	Number	Double 2dp
Date of Birth	Date/Time	Short Date
Fee	Number	Long Integer

Table 4.3 The design of the Actors table

15   Start Access and create a new database. Call it **Actors**.
16   Create a new table in Design view. Enter the field names, data types and field sizes or formats.
17   Save the table as **Actors(your name)**. Do not let Access create a primary key.
18   Switch to Datasheet view and enter the data given in the original draft table of data.
19   Print a copy of the table on one sheet of paper. Write **Printout 1** in pen on the printout.

Information: Creating a table in Access

Access provides three ways of creating a table. You should always create tables in Design view. It is important to get the table design right before entering the data. Suitable choices of fields and data types help to make an efficient database that does all that is required of it. Poor choices of fields and data types can lead to a database that performs badly and cannot do what is needed. When you create a table in Design view, you are forced to think about the fields and data types that you are using.

Access will allow you to create a table by entering data straight away. It will give the fields temporary names of Field1, Field2, etc. It will guess what data type is needed, depending on what sort of data you key in. Do not use this method. Design your tables for yourself.

The third method is to use the table wizard. You may like to experiment with this wizard if you have spare time, but the tables it creates are not suitable for City & Guilds work. If you want to catalogue your household goods, your video collection or the plants in your garden then the wizard may help you create a suitable table.

Information: Choice of data types

You have already set data types in Design view of a table several times, but here is a summary of the main settings you are likely to use at Level 1.

Text

A field with the Text data type can contain any combination of characters: letters, numbers, spaces or punctuation. The field size is the number of characters the field can store. The default field size is 50 but you can choose any size up to 255 characters. Choose a size that is larger than the maximum number of characters you expect. If you need more than 255 characters then choose the **Memo** field type instead of text.

Number

A field with the Number data type can hold whole numbers such as 82 or 3487. It can hold numbers with a fractional or decimal part, such as 3.45 or 783.903. It can hold negative numbers such as –4 or –5.32. It cannot hold letters, spaces or punctuation marks other than a single decimal point. You can format numbers to display commas separating the thousands or currency symbols such as £ or the euro sign €, though these symbols are not stored as part of the number. Choose a Number data type if the numbers are to be used for calculations or sorted in number order.

If you choose the Number data type, then you must also choose a suitable field size. Here are the main field sizes available for numbers:

Byte	whole numbers up to 255
Integer	whole numbers up to 32767
Long Integer	whole numbers up to 2,147,483,647
Single	numbers with up to 7 decimal places
Double	numbers with up to 15 decimal places.

Use Long Integer for whole numbers and use Double for numbers with decimal places unless storage space is a problem. The databases that you produce for your City & Guilds work are small, so that there is no need to worry about saving storage space.

You can use the Format and Decimal Places properties to control the way the number is displayed. To show two decimal places, you set Format to Fixed and Decimal Places to 2.

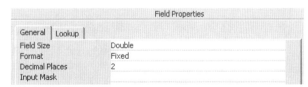

Figure 4.1 Setting 2 decimal places

To show a £ sign but no decimal places, you set Format to Currency and Decimal Places to 0.

Figure 4.2 Setting currency with 0 decimal places

Currency

Currency is a variation of the Number data type. It is suitable if you want to show amounts of money with the £ sign and 2 decimal places. It is designed for fast and efficient calculation. If you want to show the £ sign and a whole number of pounds then you could use Currency and choose 0 decimal places, or you could use the Number data type and choose Long Integer as shown in Figure 4.2. At Level 1, with small databases, it does not matter whether you choose Currency or Number as long as the display is correct. The choice becomes important when people design large databases that need to be efficient.

Date/Time

This is the type to choose for dates and times. You can choose the format of a Date/Time field to show a date as Short Date, e.g. 12/09/02, or as Medium Date, e.g. 12-Sep-02, or as Long Date, e.g. 12 September 2002.

AutoNumber

AutoNumber is a special kind of Long Integer. It automatically enters numbers for you so that your first record is number 1, your next record is number 2, and so on.

Information: Primary key

You are not expected to create a primary key for a table at Level 1. Primary keys are introduced here because you might like an explanation of the message you see when you save the design of a table, 'There is no primary key defined'.

A primary key field has a different entry in each record. It is used to identify each record uniquely. Look at the table of employees.

Surname	Initials	Title	Branch	StartDate	Salary	Payroll No	BirthDate
Hussein	M	Cashier	Exeter	01/02/80	15000	309	19/02/69
Watson	P	Manager	Exeter	01/03/82	28000	311	31/05/63
Shah	P	Manager	Bradford	01/06/85	26000	305	21/08/62
Evans	K	Cashier	Newbury	01/04/89	14600	312	04/10/52
Smith	T	IT Technician	Leeds	01/02/01	10000	313	14/08/82
Smith	M	Cashier	Reading	02/09/02	11500	316	05/08/81
Lee	C	Cashier	Leeds	02/09/02	11500	315	23/09/80

Table 4.4 Part of the Employees table

The Surname field could not be used as a primary key because people might share the same surname. Similarly, people might share the same initials, title, branch, start date, salary or date of birth. Only the Payroll No is certain to be different for each person. Payroll No could be a primary key for the table. →

Unique identifiers or codes are commonly used in everyday life. Each person of working age has a National Insurance number. Each bank account has a number. Each item in a catalogue has a catalogue number. Each car has a registration number. Each published book has an ISBN number. These identifiers are likely to make suitable primary keys for tables.

Primary keys are useful in large tables and they are necessary when tables are linked together. If a table has no suitable primary key field then an extra identifier field can be added. Access offers to create an extra field for you when you save a table without a primary key. At Level 1, remember to say No to this offer. If you say Yes, then you will find an extra unwanted field in your table.

Task 4.2 — Insert a new field

It is easy to add a field to the end of a table as you did in Task 2.4 of Section 2. You go to Design view of the table and put in the new field at the end of the list of fields. The agent for the actors wants an extra field called Code No in the Actors table, but asks for the extra field to be the second field, not the last field. You will need to insert the new field into the list of fields.

Method

1   Start with your Actors table on the screen in Datasheet view. It should contain the records as shown in Table 4.1 at the start of this section.
2   Switch to Design view of the Actors table.
3   Click into the second row of the list of fields to select it. This should be the Experience field. A black triangle should appear in the left margin.
4   Click on the Insert menu to show the drop down list. Select Rows.

Hint:

Another way of inserting a row is to click the Insert Rows button on the toolbar.

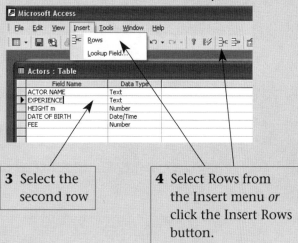

3 Select the second row

4 Select Rows from the Insert menu *or* click the Insert Rows button.

Figure 4.3 Inserting a row

5   A new row should appear between Actor Name and Experience.
6   Key in the new field name **CODE NO**.
7   Choose Number as the data type of the field.
8   Keep the default Long Integer as the field size in the lower part of the window.
9   Save the table structure by clicking the Save button on the toolbar.
10 Switch to Datasheet view of the table. Give each actor a code number as follows:

ACTOR NAME	CODE NO
Seymore Anya	1
Clarke Chris	2
Raven Damon	3
Prince Paula	4
Carston Craig	5
Bayliss Lauren	6
Mayne Meriel	7
Jackson Wayne	8

Table 4.5 Code Numbers for the Actors table

Task 4.3 | Delete a field

The Fee field is no longer needed. The agent wants it to be deleted.

Method

1. Switch to Design view of the Actors table.
2. Click into the Fee row to select it.
3. Click the Edit menu to show the drop down list and select Delete Rows.

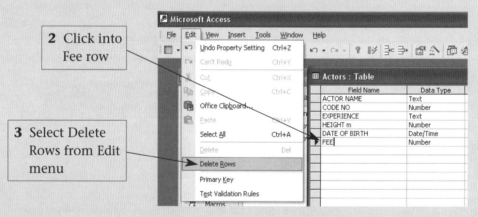

Figure 4.4 Deleting a row

4. A message should appear, saying: 'Do you want to permanently delete the selected field(s) and all the data in the field(s)?' This is an important warning. If you go ahead and delete the field, then you will not be able to get the data back. In this case we are sure that the data will not be needed again. Click on Yes to delete the field.
5. Save the table design.
6. Switch to Datasheet view to see the new version of the table.
7. Print the table on one sheet of paper. Write **Printout 2** in pen on the printout. It should look like Table 4.6.

ACTOR NAME	CODE NO	EXPERIENCE	HEIGHT m	DATE OF BIRTH
Seymore Anya	1	Film	1.70	12/12/76
Clarke Chris	2	Film	1.85	02/07/81
Raven Damon	3	TV	1.80	05/09/78
Prince Paula	4	Stage	1.63	01/04/80
Carston Craig	5	TV	1.79	14/08/79
Bayliss Lauren	6	TV	1.68	25/04/81
Mayne Meriel	7	Film	1.66	28/02/79
Jackson Wayne	8	Stage	1.89	16/03/75

Table 4.6 The altered Actors table

Task 4.4 — Increase field size

When you set up the Actor Name field, you gave it a field length of 40 characters. This is a generous length. It could even hold 'The artist formerly known as Prince'. It is possible that a field size may need to be changed to allow for exceptionally long entries. Suppose that Meriel Mayne changes her name to 'Meriel the incredible star of the silver screen Mayne'. She now has a name of 53 characters. She has no consideration for the poor database user. You will need to increase the field size.

Method

1   Start with your Actors table on the screen in Datasheet view.
2   Try to change the entry 'Mayne Meriel' to 'Mayne Meriel the incredible star of the silver screen'. You should find that you can get as far as the second 'the', but the field will not accept any more characters. Making the field wider in the display does not help. Only 40 characters can be stored in the field.
3   Switch to Design view.
4   Change the field size of the Actor Name field to 60.
5   Save the table design.
6   Switch to Datasheet view.
7   Continue keying in Meriel's name. This time it should all fit in the field.

Task 4.5 — Decrease field size

This change of name has turned out to be such a nuisance that the actress changes her name back to plain 'Meriel Mayne'. You decide to change the field size back to 40.

Method

1. Switch to Design view of the Actors table.
2. Change the field size of the Actor Name field to 40.
3. Save the table design.
4. You should see a warning message, 'Some data may be lost', explaining that a field size has been made smaller and that this may give problems. Click Yes to continue with the save.
5. Switch to Datasheet view.
6. The last part of Meriel's name has been lost as the warning message said. Edit the entry back to the original 'Mayne Meriel'.
7. Close your Actors table and close down Access.

Hint:

You can always make a text field bigger up to the limit of 255 characters. Be very cautious about making a text field smaller. You may lose data.

→ Practise your skills 1: Catering

A catering firm supplies buffets and sit-down meals. You are asked to create a database to hold records of orders.

Customer name	Phone	Event	Date	No of guests	Price per guest
Briggs M	01889 232456	Wedding	04/10/02	200	£8.50
Naylor H	01889 287901	18th birthday	08/10/02	50	£6.75
Pargeter J	01889 277300	Wedding	15/10/02	150	£10.00
Okole M	01889 222739	Wedding	20/10/02	180	£10.00
Carson F	01889 218112	Anniversary	21/10/02	50	£13.50

Table 4.7 Data for the Catering table

1 Start to design the table on paper. Make three columns headed Field name, Data type and Field size/format. Write down the field names in the first column.

2 Decide on a suitable data type for each field and write it into your design. Decide on a suitable field size or format for each field and write it in.

3 Start Access and create a new database called Catering.

4 Create a new table according to your design. Save the table as Catering and add your own name in brackets.

5 Enter the records.

6 Print the table on one sheet of paper. Write Printout 1 on the printout.

7 The firm now asks for some changes. Add a new field between the Event and Date fields. Give it the field name **Order**. It should be a text field, size 20.

8 Enter data in the new field as follows:

Customer name	Order
Briggs M	Buffet A
Naylor H	Buffet B
Pargeter J	Sit-down B
Okole M	Sit-down B
Carson F	Sit-down A

Table 4.8 Data for the Order field

9 Delete the Price per Guest field.

10 Increase the field size of the Order field to 40.

11 Change J Pargeter's order to **Sit-down B with special order cake**.

12 Reduce the size of the Event field to 12.

13 Print the table on one sheet of paper. Write Printout 2 on the printout.

14 Restore the Event field to its original size and re-enter any lost data.

15 Close the table and close down Access.

→ Practise your skills 2: Coach travel

A bus and coach company are offering special rates on travel to major towns and cities on certain days in June. You are asked to create a database to hold the data.

Destination	Date	Time (hours)	Fare	Type
Manchester	11-Jun-02	1.5	£9.00	return
Bradford	13-Jun-02	0.5	£2.25	return
Birmingham	13-Jun-02	3.5	£21.50	return
Bristol	14-Jun-02	6.0	£39.00	return
Carlisle	16-Jun-02	4.0	£20.00	return
Cardiff	20-Jun-02	6.5	£39.00	return

Table 4.9 Data for the coach table

1 Start to design the table on paper. Make three columns headed Field name, Data type and Field size/format. Write down the field names in the first column.

2 Decide on a suitable data type for each field and write it into your design. Decide on a suitable field size or format for each field and write it in.

3 Start Access and create a new database called Coach travel.

4 Create a new table according to your design. Save the table as Travel and add your own name in brackets.

5 Enter the records.

6 Print the table on one sheet of paper. Write Printout 1 on the printout.

7 The company now asks for some changes. Add a new field after the Date field and call it Return. It should have a type suitable for holding the return date.

8 Enter data in the new field as follows:

Destination	Date	Return
Manchester	11-Jun-02	11-Jun-02
Bradford	13-Jun-02	13-Jun-02
Birmingham	13-Jun-02	14-Jun-02
Bristol	14-Jun-02	15-Jun-02
Carlisle	16-Jun-02	17-Jun-02
Cardiff	20-Jun-02	21-Jun-02

Table 4.10 Data for the Return field

9 Delete the Type field.

10 The Time (hours) field should already be showing 1 decimal place. Change the format so that it shows 2 decimal places.

11 Change the format of the dates so that they show in the form 11/6/02 instead of 11-Jun-02.

12 Print the table on one sheet of paper. Write Printout 2 on the printout.

13 Close the table and close down Access.

→ Check your knowledge

1 What is an integer?

2 What data type and field size should you choose for a field to hold numbers that have fractional (decimal) parts?

3 What data type is usually suitable for a field to hold phone numbers?

4 Why should you not format a Long Integer field to show 2 decimal places?

5 Is there a field in the Actors table that would be suitable as a primary key? If so, which field?

6 Is there a field in the Travel table that would be suitable as a primary key? If so, which field?

A local charity wants a database to store records of its regular donors. They ask you to set up such a database. They give you a sample of the data.

Donor No	Surname	Initials	Amount	Frequency	Started
1	Aldridge	H S	£100.00	Annual	01/04/99
2	Adjei	A	£80.00	Annual	01/06/00
3	Ash	C	£10.00	Monthly	01/01/98
4	Aziz	K	£10.00	Monthly	01/03/01
5	Austin	G K	£50.00	Annual	01/04/99
6	Ashby-Crumm	F	£5.50	Monthly	01/04/98
7	Andrews	M	£5.00	Monthly	01/08/99
8	Ali	S	£10.00	Monthly	01/02/99
9	Abernethy	B	£50.00	Annual	01/07/01
10	Avery	D S	£8.00	Monthly	01/10/98
11	Ashraf	M	£5.50	Monthly	01/02/02
12	Asquith	B	£6.50	Monthly	01/06/99
13	Akerman	S	£10.00	Monthly	01/04/02

Table 4.11 Data for the Donors table

1 Design the table, choosing a suitable data type and field size or format for each field.

2 Create a new database called Charity.

3 Create a new table according to your design. Save the table as Donors.

4 Enter the records.

5 Print the table on one sheet of paper. Write Printout 1 on the printout.

6 Print out all the records, sorted in order of the starting date. Write Printout 2 on the printout.

7 Print out the records of people who make monthly donations, sorted in order of amount of payment. Write Printout 3 on the printout.

8 Print out the records of people who started making donations before 01/01/00. Sort in order of surname and show the Surname, Amount and Frequency fields only. Write Printout 4 on the printout.

9 Add an extra field called **Special Appeal**. This field is to hold the additional amount of money donated to a special one-off appeal.

10 Enter data into the new field as follows:

Donor No	Surname	Special Appeal
1	Aldridge	£20.00
2	Adjei	£15.00
3	Ash	£0.00
4	Aziz	£15.00
5	Austin	£5.50
6	Ashby-Crumm	£20.00
7	Andrews	£2.50
8	Ali	£20.00
9	Abernethy	£15.00
10	Avery	£0.00
11	Ashraf	£0.00
12	Asquith	£7.50
13	Akerman	£0.00

Table 4.12 Data for the Special Appeal field

11 Add three extra records to the table.

Donor No	Surname	Initials	Amount	Frequency	Started	Special Appeal
14	Adams	E	£10.00	Monthly	01/05/02	£0.00
15	Appleford	C	£7.50	Monthly	01/05/02	£0.00
16	Austin	N W	£200.00	Annual	01/06/02	£0.00

Table 4.13 Extra records for the Donors table

12 D S Avery is no longer a donor. Delete the record.

13 S Akerman has increased the monthly donation to £12.50. Alter the record.

14 Print the records of donors who gave less than £5 to the special appeal. Show all fields and sort in order of donor number. The printout should be on one sheet of paper. Write Printout 5 on the printout.

15 Close down Access.

You will learn to

- Create a suitably named directory to be used as a location for backup copies of the data files/tables
- Make backup copies of the data files/tables using filenames which identify them as backup copies, storing them in a suitably identified location
- Save files to floppy disk

Information

Backup copies

A backup copy of a file is a second copy that can be used if the first copy is damaged or lost. Disk storage is usually fairly reliable, but occasionally disks do become faulty so that some or all of the files on them can no longer be used. Computer users sometimes delete files by mistake. Files can also be damaged or deleted by virus action. If an up-to-date backup copy exists then a file can be replaced. If there is no backup copy then the data may be lost for ever.

Any business organisation that uses a database must take steps to back up the database file at regular intervals. The back up may take place daily or at some other interval, depending on how often the database is altered. It must always be possible to restore the most up-to-date state of the database.

Backup copies are usually made on removable disks or on special tape. They should be kept securely in a fireproof data safe in a place away from the original copy. Suppose the computer building were destroyed by fire. A computer and even a building can be replaced, the database can be restored from the backup, and the organisation can survive. If there were no backup, the loss of the database of customer and sales information would almost certainly mean the end of the organisation.

Your own computer files may not be vital to your survival, but even so it is a good idea for you to keep backup copies of your work. For home use, floppy disks are useful for storing backup copies of small files. Recordable or rewritable CDs are becoming popular for storing large files or large numbers of files. Other types of disks, such as zip disks, are also available, but becoming less popular.

Files

Everything that is stored on disks is stored as files. There are two main kinds of files. Data files include all the work that you and other computer users produce. Word processed documents, spreadsheets, databases, web pages, graphic images, sounds and video clips are all saved as data files. System files hold the programs and related information that the computer needs in order to work.

You learned in Section 1 that files have names in two parts, separated by a dot. The part after the dot is the extension, and tells the computer system what kind of data is stored in the file. Access creates its database files with the .mdb extension. Other important extensions for data files include:

.doc   a Word document
.xls   an Excel spreadsheet
.txt   a plain text file
.bmp   a bitmapped graphic image file

System files also have extensions. A program file that is ready to run usually has the .exe extension. Other system file extensions include .com, .ini, .sys and .dll. Do not delete system files or the computer may stop working properly.

Files may be displayed on the screen as icons as shown in Figure 5.1. Different kinds of files have different icons. Access 2000 and Access 2002 .mdb files are shown with a red key. Older versions of Access use a yellow key instead. The extensions may or may not be shown. It depends on how the system has been set up. Alternatively, files may be displayed as a list as shown in Figure 5.2.

Figure 5.1 Files shown as icons

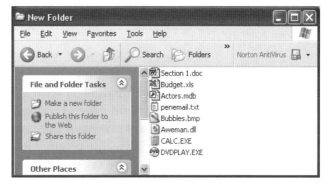

Figure 5.2 Files shown as a list

It is usually possible to open a data file by double clicking on its icon. Windows will start up the appropriate program to manage the file, and then open the data file.

Directories (Folders)

A disk might hold hundreds or thousands of files. For convenience, the files need to be organised so that they can easily be found and managed. Files are therefore grouped into directories or folders. Directory is the older and more general name. Recent versions of Windows use the name folder instead. Folders (or subdirectories) can be placed inside other folders to create a filing system on many levels. Figure 5.3 shows database files stored in a folder called Access Databases. This folder is in another folder called My Documents, and My Documents is stored on Drive C, which is the hard disk of the computer. Notice that the Access Databases folder has an icon showing that it is open. The other folders have icons showing that they are closed.

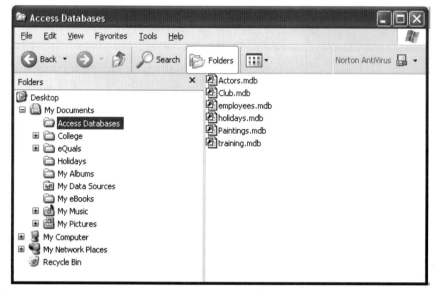

Figure 5.3 Files and Folders

Task 5.1   Create a suitably named directory to be used as a location for backup copies of the data files/tables

In Task 1.4 of Section 1, you created a new folder (directory) to hold your database files. You did this from inside the Access application. This time you will be working directly with Windows and not inside Access. The details of the method will depend on how your computer has been set up and where you normally save your files. At first you will be making a backup folder on the same disk as the original folder. This is not ideal, but it is useful practice. Later you will be saving backup copies to a different disk.

There are different versions of Windows, and each can be customised to display folders and files in different ways. The descriptions are of Windows XP. Your system may not look like the illustrations, but it should be possible to carry out similar actions.

Method

1   Start with your Windows desktop on the screen. You do not need Access or any other applications open.
2   Click the Start button. If you are at home, the start menu should include options called 'My Documents' and 'My Computer'. If you are working on a network in a college, school or training centre, there may be slightly different options, but one of these options should be for the area where you keep your files.

3 Point your mouse to the 'My Computer' option, and a sub-menu should appear on the right of the main menu. Do not click yet.

Figure 5.4 The Start menu

4 'My Computer' shows the storage areas available on your computer. Figure 5.4 shows one floppy disk drive (A:), one hard disk drive (C:), one DVD drive (D:) and one CD drive (E:). Your computer may have a different set of drives. If you are working on a networked computer, you may see one or more network drives listed. The list also includes the main folders used for storing files created by different users of the computer.

5 If you want to create, move or delete folders and organise your files, then 'My Computer' is a good place to start. If you want to find and open an existing file then it is probably easier and quicker to start by pointing the mouse to 'My Documents' in order to see a list of your files and folders within the main 'My Documents' folder. Point your mouse to 'My Documents' to see what is on your list, but do not click.

Figure 5.5 Start menu showing My Documents

6   Point your mouse to 'My Computer' again. This time point the mouse to the 'My Documents' option on the submenu and click. (If the folder containing your files has a different name on your computer system, then click on that name instead.) A new window opens showing your files and folders inside 'My Documents'.

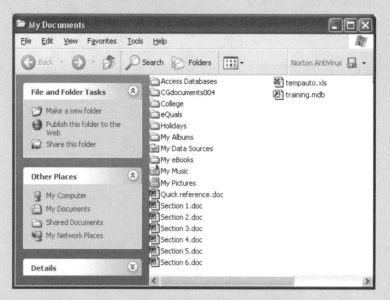

Figure 5.6 Window showing contents of My Documents folder

There may be a shortcut on your desktop to the folder containing your work. If there is such a shortcut then you can double click it to open the folder. This is quicker than going in step by step, starting with My Computer.

Figure 5.7 Shortcut to My Documents

7   In Section 1 you created the Access Databases folder inside the My Documents folder. You should see the Access Databases folder listed in your My Documents window. You created this folder from within Access. Next you will create another new folder, using the Windows operating system directly, and not using Access.

8   Click the File menu at the top of your window so that the drop down list is shown. Select New from the drop down list. A second list appears. Select Folder.

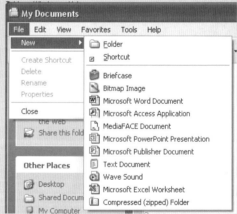

Figure 5.8 Creating a new folder

9   A new folder appears in the window. It has the default name 'New Folder'. The name is highlighted so that you can key in a new name to replace the old name. Key in the new name: **Backup databases**.

Make backup copies of the data files/tables using filenames which identify them as backup copies, storing them in a suitably identified location

Hint:

You can move a window on the screen. Point the mouse to the title bar of the window. Hold down the left mouse button and drag the window to its new position.

You will make a second copy of your Actors database and store it in your Backup Databases folder There are many ways of doing this. The following method is not the quickest, but it does allow you to see what is happening at each step.

Method

1. Start with your My Documents folder window showing on the screen. Double click on the Access Databases folder so that it opens in its own window. You should be able to see your Actors database in the list of files.
2. Your My Documents folder window may or may not still be showing. This depends on how your system has been set up. If it is not still showing, you need to show it again. Click the Start button, select My Computer, then select My Documents.
3. In the My Documents window, double click on the Backup Databases folder so that it opens its own windows. Arrange the Access Databases and the Backup Databases windows so that they are displayed side by side on the screen. See Figure 5.9.

Figure 5.9 Backup and Access Databases folders

4. Click on the name of the Actors.mdb database file to select it.
5. Click on the Edit menu in the Access Databases window to show the drop down list, and select Copy.
6. Click on the Edit menu in the Backup Databases window to show the drop down list and select Paste. A copy of the Actors.mdb file should appear in the Backup databases window.
7. Right click on the name of this copy of the file. A pop-up menu should show. Select Rename from the menu.
8. Change the name of the file to ActorsBackup.mdb.
9. Close each window by clicking the X button in the top right corner.

Information: choosing names for backup files

A backup copy of a file should have a name that shows it is a backup copy of a file, and shows which file has been backed up. There are two ways to name backup files. One is to keep the name the same, but change the extension to .bak. This has the disadvantage that Windows cannot tell what kind of file it is and will not know which application to use to open it. Windows gives you a warning message if you change the extension of a file. You would need to change the extension back yourself if you wanted to use the file. The other way is to keep the extension the same, but change the name. This is the approach you used in Task 5.2. In a City & Guilds test, you may be asked to use a specific name for a backup file, or you may be left to choose a suitable name for yourself.

Task 5.3 — Copy files to floppy disk

You are probably saving your files on a hard disk. This may be the hard disk in the computer you are using. If you are using a networked computer, it may be a hard disk on a central computer. Hard disks are most convenient for normal working. When you hand in files for marking, and particularly when you do an assignment, your tutor may ask you to save a file to a floppy disk, sometimes called a diskette. Floppy disks are removable, and can be used in another computer. They can also be stored in case your work needs to be checked later. Floppy disks are also useful for making backup copies of files.

For this task you will need a floppy disk, labelled and ready to use.

Hint:

There is another way of copying the file to the new folder than the one shown in Task 5.2. Hold down the Ctrl key on the keyboard as you use the mouse to drag the file across to the new folder. Release the mouse before you release the Ctrl key. Check that there is a copy of the file in both folders. If you do not hold the Ctrl key down, the file will be moved instead of copied and the original version will be lost.

Method

1 Start with your Windows desktop showing on the screen.
2 Put the floppy disk in its drive. The label should be uppermost. You should hold the disk label so that the metal slider goes into the drive first. Push the disk in until you hear a click.

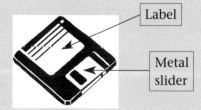

Figure 5.10 Floppy disk

You can copy a whole folder using copy and paste in the same way as you can copy a file. You can also drag a folder from one window to another. Try copying the complete Backup Databases folder to the floppy disk.

3   Click the Start button and point the mouse to My Computer.
4   Click on the menu option $3\frac{1}{2}$ floppy (A:).
5   A window should open to display the contents of the floppy disk. If there are no files on the disk then the window will be empty.
6   Create a folder on the floppy disk by clicking on the File menu and selecting New then Folder from the drop down lists. You should see the floppy disk drive light go on as the disk is used.
7   Rename your new folder as **Database Backup 2**.
8   Double click on your new folder to open it.
9   Starting from the Start button, find and open your Access Databases folder so that the list of files is displayed in a window.
10 Copy your Actors.mdb file from the Access Databases folder and paste it into the Database Backup 2 folder. Use Edit – Copy and Edit – Paste as you did in the previous task. The copying will take longer this time, because floppy disks work more slowly than hard disks. Again you should see the drive light go on as the disk works.
11 Rename the Actors.mdb file in the backup folder. Call it ActorsBackup.mdb.
12 Close the windows.
13 When you have finished with the floppy disk, make sure that the drive light is off, then press the button on the disk drive. The disk will pop out so that you can remove it.

→ Practise your skills 1: Holiday backup

1   Create a new folder called Holidays inside your Access Databases folder.
2   Move your holidays.mdb database file into the Holidays folder.
3   Create a new folder called Hbackup inside your Backup Databases folder.
4   Copy your holidays.mdb database file to the Hbackup folder. Make sure that the original file is still in the Holidays folder.
5   Change the name of the copy to holidaysbackup.mdb.
6   Create a new folder called Hbackup2 on a floppy disk.
7   Put a copy of your holidays.mdb database file in the Hbackup2 folder. Call the copy holidaysbackup2.mdb.
8   Close all windows.
9   Start up Access. Find and open your holidaysbackup.mdb file and make sure that it contains a working copy of your database.
10 Close Access.

Hint:

You can select and copy several files at the same time. Hold down the Ctrl key as you click on the files to select them.

→ **Practise your skills 2: More backup**

1 Copy all your remaining databases to your Backup Databases folder.

→ **Check your knowledge**

1 What is the other name for a folder?

2 Suggest three ways in which files may be damaged or lost.

3 Why should backup copies be made?

4 Name three kinds of removable disks that could be used for backup.

5 What sort of file has the .exe extension?

6 Disk drives are given letters to identify them. A computer's main or only hard disk drive is given the letter C:. What letter is given to the floppy disk drive?

Practice assignments

In order to achieve the Level 1 database qualification, you need to take and pass one assignment. There are Pass, Credit and Distinction grades available. Your tutor will give you the real assignment when you and your tutor agree that you are ready.

You will be producing printed work. Your tutor will also need to check your saved files. Your tutor will tell you where you should save your files. This may be in a special network area or it may be on a floppy disk.

Practice assignment 1

You are advised to read all instructions carefully before starting work and to check with your assessor, if necessary, to ensure that you have fully understood what is required.

You must, at all times, observe all relevant health and safety precautions.

Time allowed: 1½ hours

> **Scenario**
> You work in a shop that sells posters of famous paintings. You have been asked to set up and maintain a database to hold information about the paintings and the posters you sell.

Tasks

1 Create two new directories called SHOP and SHOPBACKUP.
2 Initiate the database application software.
3 Create a new database called PAINTINGS and save it in the directory called SHOP.
4 Create a database structure for paintings as shown below.

Field name	Data type	Field length
Painting	Text	30
Artist	Text	20
Height cm	Number/Integer	
Width cm	Number/Integer	
Location	Text	25
Poster price	Number/Currency	

Table 6.1 Structure of the Paintings table

5 Enter the following records.

Painting	Artist	Height cm	Width cm	Location	Poster price
Marshy Landscape	Rousseau	22	28	private	£12.99
Canal St Martin, Paris	Sisley	50	65	Paris	£14.99
Rough Sea, Etretat	Monet	81	100	Lyon	£19.99
Mario Ochard	Monet	32	24	Chicago	£12.99
The River	Monet	40	50	Paris	£14.99
The Pedicure	Degas	61	46	Paris	£14.99
Dulwich College	Pissaro	50	61	Winnipeg	£16.99
At the Seaside	Degas	47	82	London	£16.99
Piazza San Marco	Sickert	16	20	Newcastle	£12.99

Table 6.2 Data for the Paintings table

6 Print out all the records in the database. Label this Printout 1.

7 Search for all paintings by Monet and print out all the records that meet this condition. Label this Printout 2.

8 Delete the Location field. Add a field named **Year** to the record structure. This field should be integer.

9 Enter the following data in the Year field.

Painting	Year
Marshy Landscape	1842
Canal St Martin, Paris	1870
Rough Sea, Etretat	1883
Mario Ochard	1858
The River	1868
The Pedicure	1873
Dulwich College	1871
At the Seaside	1876
Piazza San Marco	1903

Table 6.3 Data for the Year field

10 Add an extra record as follows:

Painting	Artist	Height cm	Width cm	Poster price	Year
Carriage at the Races	Degas	36	55	£12.99	1873

Table 6.4 Extra record for the Paintings table

11 Sort the records in ascending order of the Year field and print out all the records in the sorted order. Label this Printout 3.

12 The poster of Dulwich College by Pissaro is no longer available. Delete the record.

13 Search for posters with a price greater than or equal to £16.99, and print out all the records that meet this condition. Label this Printout 4.

14 The price of the poster of Rough Sea, Etretat by Monet has been reduced to £18.50. Alter the record to show the new price.

15 Print out all the records including only the fields Painting, Artist and Poster price. Label this Printout 5.

16 Search for posters with a width of less than 50 cm. Print out all the records that meet this condition including only the fields Painting, Height cm and Width cm. Label this Printout 6.

17 Save and exit the database.

18 Copy all the files for the database into the SHOPBACKUP directory.

19 Rename the files in the SHOPBACKUP directory to clearly identify them as backup files.

20 Hand in your printouts to the assessor.

Note:

- At the conclusion of this assignment, hand in all paperwork and disks to the test supervisor.
- Ensure that your name is on the disk (if using a floppy disk) and all documentation.
- If the assignment is taken over more than one period, all floppy disks and paperwork must be returned to the test supervisor at the end of each sitting.

Practice assignment 2

You are advised to read all instructions carefully before starting work and to check with your assessor, if necessary, to ensure that you have fully understood what is required.

You must, at all times, observe all relevant health and safety precautions.

Time allowed: 1½ hours

> **Scenario**
>
> You work in the office of Hayscastle Leisure Centre. The leisure centre has decided to computerise its membership records. You have been requested to set up and maintain a database and provide information to the Manager.

Tasks

1 Create two new directories called LEISURE and LEISUREBACKUP.

2 Initiate the database application software.

3 Create a new database called MEMBERS and save it in the directory called LEISURE.

4 Create a database structure for members as shown below.

Field name	Data type	Field length
Member No	Numeric/Integer	
Last Name	Text	20
First Name	Text	20
Address	Text	30
Town	Text	25
Postcode	Text	15
Date joined	Date	

Table 6.5 Structure of the Members table

5 Enter the following records.

Member No	Last Name	First Name	Address	Town	Postcode	Date Joined
98	Avery	Pamela	142 Holmes Road	HAYSCASTLE	HY6 3WX	14/12/92
99	Lai	Sally	3 Kidlington Road	WOODFORD	WO2 7SH	12/03/97
100	Thorpe	Marianne	213 Woking Road	HAYSCASTLE	HY6 2GN	03/02/97
101	Jackson	Peter	36 Cumnor Gardens	HAYSCOT	HY11 4GN	18/07/99
102	Hope	James	14 Beaver Close	WOODFORD	WO3 9BN	02/08/96
103	Otway	Charles	18 East Road	HAYSCOT	HY11 1HJ	03/03/00
104	Cantwell	Rachel	5 Grant Avenue	HAYSCOT	HY11 7SN	06/05/99
105	Al-Amri	Hussein	12 Belle Avenue	HAYSCASTLE	HY2 9SM	12/05/99
106	Johnston	Frances	4 Holliwell Road	WOODFORD	WO4 8SJ	18/10/00
107	Wilde	Paul	74 Cowley Road	WOODFORD	WO4 6SM	30/01/00

Table 6.6 Data for the Members table

6 Print out all the records in the database. Label this Printout 1.

7 Search for all members who live in Woodford and print out all the records that meet this condition. Label this Printout 2.

8 Add a field named **Payment** to the record structure. This field should be Currency, 2 decimal places.

9 Enter the following data in the Payment field.

Member No	Payment
98	£165.50
99	£238.00
100	£210.00
101	£238.00
102	£165.50
103	£210.00
104	£165.50
105	£210.00
106	£210.00
107	£210.00

Table 6.7 Data for the Payment field

10 Sort the records in ascending order of the Last Name field and print out all the records in the sorted order. Label this Printout 3.

11 Charles Otway is no longer a member. Delete his record.

12 Search for members whose payment is less than or equal to £210.00, and print out all the records that meet this condition. Label this Printout 4.

13 Marianne Thorpe has moved house. Change her address to 15 Holmes Road. The town stays the same. Change her postcode to HY6 3WN.

14 Print out all the records including only the fields Last Name, First Name, Address, Town and Postcode. Label this Printout 5.

15 Search for members who joined before June 1st 1999 and print out all the records that meet this condition including only the fields Last Name, First Name and Date Joined. Label this Printout 6.

16 Save and exit the database.

17 Copy all the files for the database into the LEISUREBACKUP directory.

18 Rename the files in the LEISUREBACKUP directory to clearly identify them as backup files.

19 Hand in your printouts to the assessor.

Note:

- At the conclusion of this assignment, hand in all paperwork and disks to the test supervisor.
- Ensure that your name is on the disk (if using a floppy disk) and all documentation.
- If the assignment is taken over more than one period, all floppy disks and paperwork must be returned to the test supervisor at the end of each sitting.

Solutions

Section 1 Getting started

Practise your skills 1
The printout should look like the table in Table 1.5.

Practise your skills 2
The printout should look like the table in Table 1.7.

Check your knowledge
1 record
2 fields
3 field name
4 file
5 Directory
6 **a** SO12 6GH
  c (01998)345678
  e 4563823a
7 Integer, Long Integer
8 Single, Double
9 Currency
10 Date/Time

Section 2 Using database tables

Practise your skills 1

Surname	Initials	Title	Branch	StartDate	Salary	Payroll No	BirthDate
Hussein	M	Cashier	Exeter	01/02/80	15000	309	19/02/69
Watson	P	Manager	Exeter	01/03/82	28000	311	31/05/63
Shah	P	Manager	Bradford	01/06/85	26000	305	21/08/62
Evans	K	Cashier	Newbury	01/04/89	14600	312	04/10/52
Stephens	B	Manager	Reading	01/09/90	30000	308	30/06/59
Lancaster	K	Manager	Leeds	01/11/92	26000	306	22/08/63
Adkins	N	Cashier	Reading	01/06/95	11500	303	08/10/71
Erikson	K	Cashier	Newbury	01/12/98	14500	314	30/09/58
Wheeler	P A	IT Technician	Reading	01/04/99	16500	304	06/07/68
Wilkins	D S	IT Technician	Exeter	01/12/99	16000	310	25/11/74
Adams	M B	Cashier	Leeds	01/08/00	12000	307	28/01/70
Smith	T	IT Technician	Leeds	01/02/01	10000	313	14/08/82
Smith	M	Cashier	Reading	02/09/02	11500	316	05/08/81
Lee	C	Cashier	Leeds	02/09/02	11500	015	23/09/80

Figure 7.1 Employees table after changes

Practise your skills 2

Resort	Country	Start date	Days	Price	Deposit	Airport
Lake Como	Italy	02/06/02	7	£415.00	£100.00	Milan
St Johann	Austria	14/06/02	7	£425.00	£100.00	Salzburg
Wengen	Switzerland	26/07/02	7	£439.00	£100.00	Zurich
Lake Geneva	Switzerland	17/08/02	7	£519.00	£120.00	Geneva
Alpbach	Austria	25/07/02	10	£530.00	£150.00	Innsbruck
Zermatt	Switzerland	19/07/02	7	£535.00	£150.00	Zurich
Interlaken	Switzerland	14/06/02	7	£545.00	£150.00	Zurich
Kaprun	Austria	08/08/02	14	£649.00	£175.00	Salzburg
Cortina	Italy	25/07/02	10	£750.00	£200.00	Milan
Seefeld	Austria	10/08/02	14	£820.00	£200.00	Innsbruck
Lake Constance	Germany	17/08/02	14	£1,166.00	£200.00	Zurich

Figure 7.2 Holiday table after changes

Check your knowledge

1 The black triangle shows that the record is selected.

2 The pencil shows that the record is being edited and the changes are not yet saved.

3 The asterisk means that this row is available for entering a new record.

4 Yes. Adding a field is a change to the table design and all changes to the design must be saved.

5 No. A record is automatically saved as soon as you move out of the record. There is no need to save the table.

6 Yes, you must save the table. Changing the width of a field counts as a design change even though you do it in Datasheet view.

7 Sorting in numerical order gives 7, 22, 62, 130, 700.

8 Sorting in alphabetical order gives 130, 22, 62, 7, 700.

9 The most likely cause is a space in front of the S of Smith. This would bring Smith to the top of the list in an ascending alphabetical sort.

10 Change to landscape orientation. If the table is already in landscape orientation, you might try to make the fields a little narrower.

Consolidation 1 Computers

Printout 1 of the Computers table should look like the table given in Consolidation 1.

Model	Processor (MHz)	Price	Sale date	Printer	Type
Advent 7003	2000	£1,799.00	08-Jun-02	N	Laptop
Net a2000 Pro	2000	£990.00	09-Jun-02	Y	Desktop
Advent 3979 BTO	1800	£939.20	10-Jun-02	N	Desktop
Holly KA 1.7	1700	£988.99	08-Jun-02	Y	Desktop
eMachines 540	1300	£904.50	11-Jun-02	Y	Desktop
Tiny Home Plus 1000	1000	£599.00	14-Jun-02	N	Desktop
HP Vectra XE310	1000	£609.83	12-Jun-02	N	Desktop
NEC Powermate	1000	£569.99	05-Jun-02	Y	Desktop
Compaq Evo N160	933	£809.58	14-Jun-02	N	Laptop
eMachines 130 CD	900	£449.00	10-Jun-02	N	Desktop

Figure 7.3 Printout 2 of Computers table

Computers with the same processor speed may be displayed in a different order.

Printout 3 of Computers table should have the same records, sorted in order of model.

Printout 4 should show only the record for the NEC Powermate.

Section 3 Database queries

Practise your skills 1

Sorted by surname: records should appear in order of surname, starting with Adams and ending with Wilkins.

Cashiers sorted by salary, descending: Hussein, Evans, Erikson, Adams, Smith, Lee, Adkins.

Staff earning £11500, sorted by birth date: Adkins, Lee, Smith.

Staff starting before 01/01/00: Hussein, Watson, Shah, Evans, Stephens, Lancaster, Adkins, Erikson, Wheeler, Wilkins.

Staff earning £14500 or more, sorted by Branch: Shah, Watson, Wilkins, Hussein, Lancaster, Erikson, Evans, Stephens, Wheeler.

Practise your skills 2

Holidays sorted alphabetically by resort start with Alpbach and end with Zermatt.

Holidays in Switzerland, sorted by price: Wengen, Lake Geneva, Zermatt, Interlaken.

7-day holidays sorted by resort name: Interlaken, Lake Como, Lake Geneva, St Johann, Wengen, Zermatt.

Holidays costing less than £600, sorted by starting date: Lake Como, St Johann, Interlaken, Zermatt, Alpbach, Wengen, Lake Geneva.

Holidays starting on or after 25/07/02, sorted by airport: Lake Geneva, Seefeld, Alpbach, Cortina, Kaprun, Lake Constance, Wengen.

Check your knowledge

1 Table.
2 Query.
3 You can save the sorting instructions in a query and use it as many times as you need. Sorting in a table will be lost when you do a different sort.
4 Double quotes should appear round Austria, to show that it is recognised as text.
5 Nothing should appear round 7. It is recognised as a number.
6 Hash marks should appear, and the entry should show as #08/08/02#.
7 >=10 in the Days field.
8 <S in the Resort field.
9 <29/07/02 in the Start date field. Alternatively you could key in <29/7/02 or <29-Jul-02 or <29 July 2002. In each case it would appear as <#29/07/02# as soon as you press Enter.
10 Almost certainly none. **17.08.02** is not recognised as a date. It is recognised as a time, and converted to #17:08:02#, meaning 8 minutes and 2 seconds after 5 pm.

Section 4 Database structure

Practise your skills 1

Field name	Data type	Field size/format
Customer name	Text	20 (or more)
Phone	Text	15 (or more)
Event	Text	25 (or more)
Date	Date/Time	Short Date
No of guests	Number	Long Integer or Integer
Price per guest	Currency	2 decimal places

Table 7.1 Design of the Catering table

Printout 1 should look like the table given in Practise your skills 1.

Printout 2 of the Catering table should show Briggs, Naylor, Pargeter, Okole, Carson.

The letter y should be missing from 18th birthday because the Event field size is 12.

Practise your skills 2

Field name	Data type	Field size/format
Destination	Text	30 (more or less)
Date	Date/Time	Medium Date
Time (hours)	Number	Double or Single, 1 decimal place
Fare	Currency	2 decimal places
Type	Text	20 (or more)

Table 7.2 Design of the Travel table

Printout 1 of the Travel table should look like the table given in Practise your skills 2.

Printout 2 of the Travel table should still show Manchester, Bradford, Birmingham, Bristol, Carlisle, Cardiff.

Check your knowledge

1 A whole number.
2 Number, either Double or Single.
3 Text.
4 Long Integer can only store whole numbers. It cannot store decimal places. It is misleading to show decimal places because people may think that the field can store decimal places.
5 The original Actors table had no suitable primary key, but the new field, Code No, is suitable.
6 No. None of the fields are suitable. If the table needed a primary key then it would be necessary to add an extra field such as Journey number. This new field would be different for each record.

Consolidation 2: Charity gifts

Field name	Data type	Field size/format
Donor no	Number	Long Integer
Surname	Text	30
Initials	Text	5
Amount	Currency	2 decimal places
Frequency	Text	10
Started	Date/Time	Short Date

Table 7.3 A possible design for the Donors table

Printout 1 should look like the table given in Consolidation 2.

Printout 2, donors sorted by starting date, start with Ash and end with Akerman.

Printout 3, monthly donations sorted by amount, should show: Andrews, Ashraf, Ashby-Crumm, Asquith, Avery, Aziz, Ash, Ali, Akerman.

Printout 4 ,donations started before 01/01/00, should show: Aldridge, Ali, Andrews, Ash, Ashby-Crumm, Asquith, Austin, Avery.

Printout 5, donations less than £5 to special appeal, should show: Ash, Andrews, Ashraf, Akerman, Adams, Appleford, Austin.

Section 5 Directories and backup
Check your knowledge
1 Directory.
2 Disk failure, accidental deletion by the user, virus action.
3 If the original files are lost or damaged, they can be replaced using the backup files.
4 Floppy disk (diskette), CD recordable or rewritable, zip disk.
5 A program that is ready to run.
6 A:

Practice assignments

Practice assignment 1
Printout 1 is the same as the table given in the assignment instructions.

Printout 2 paintings by Monet: Rough Sea, Etretat, Mario Ochard, The River.

Printout 3 sorted by year. Start with Marshy Landscape and end with Piazza San Marco.

Printout 4, posters with a price greater than or equal to £16.99, should show Rough Sea, Etretat and At the Seaside.

Printout 5, Painting, Artist and Poster price fields. Rough Sea, Etretat should have a poster price of £18.50.

Printout 6, less than 50 cm wide, should show Marshy Landscape, Mario Ochard, The Pedicure and Piazza San Marco.

Practice assignment 2

Printout 1 is the same as the table given in the assignment instructions.

Printout 2, members living in Woodford, should show Lai, Hope, Johnston and Wilde.

Printout 3 should include the Payment field and be sorted by last name, starting with Al-Amri and finishing with Wilde.

Printout 4, payments less than or equal to £210.00, should show Avery, Thorpe, Hope, Cantwell, Al-Amri, Johnston, Wilde. The order does not matter.

Printout 5, Name and Address fields only for all 9 records. Marianne Thorpe should be at 15 Holmes Road.

Printout 6, members joined before June 1st 1999, should show Avery, Lai, Thorpe, Hope, Cantwell, Al Amri, with Last Name, First Name and Date Joined fields only.

Outcomes matching guide

All the City & Guilds outcomes for 004 Databases are covered.

Outcome 1: Create and maintain database storage locations
Outcome 2: Create a simple database
Outcome 3: Maintain a simple database
Outcome 4: Carry out single condition searches on a database
Outcome 5: Produce hard copy output

Outcome 1: Create and maintain database storage locations		
1.1	Create a suitably named directory in which to store the data files/tables	Section 1 Task 1.4
1.2	Create a suitably named directory to be used as a location for backup copies of the data files/tables	Section 5 Task 5.1
1.3	Access the database software from an operating system environment	Section 1 Task 1.2
1.4	Identify and access existing data files/tables	Section 2 Task 2.1
1.5	Make backup copies of the data files/tables using filenames which identify them as backup copies, storing them in a suitably identified location	Section 5 Task 5.2
1.6	Exit the database software ensuring all data files/tables have been saved to an appropriate location	Section 1 Task 1.15
Outcome 2: Create a simple database		
2.1	Identify common database terms: (a) database (b) table (c) field (d) record	Section 1 Information: database terms
2.2	Identify data types: (a) character or text (b) numeric (c) date (d) currency	Section 1 Information: data types
2.3	For a given database, identify the structure in terms of field names and data types	Section 2 Task 2.2
2.4	For a draft table of data, define the database structure in terms of field names and data types	Section 4 Task 4.1
2.5	Create a new database from a defined database structure	Section 1 Task 1.7
2.6	Save the database	Section 1 Task 1.8
Outcome 3: Maintain a simple database		
3.1	Open an existing database and display the records and fields for editing	Section 2 Task 2.3
3.2	Add a new record to an existing database	Section 2 Task 2.6
3.3	Add new data to a record	Section 2 Task 2.5
3.4	Edit data	Section 2 Task 2.7

3.5	Delete a record	Section 2 Task 2.8
3.6	Sort the records in a table/file in ascending or descending order: (a) alphabetical (b) numeric	Section 2 Task 2.9, 2.10
3.7	Save the modified database	Section 2 Task 2.11

Outcome 4: Carry out single condition searches on a database

4.1	Identify relational operators: (a) equals = (b) less than < (c) greater than > (d) less than or equal to <= (e) greater than or equal to >= (f) not equal to <>	Section 3 Information: relational operators
4.2	Using relational operators, execute searches on fields: • text/character • numeric • date • currency	Section 3 Task 3.13, 3.14, 3.15, 3.16

Outcome 5: Produce hard copy output

5.1	Print all the records in a table/file including all the fields	Section 1 Task 1.12, 1.13, 1.14
5.2	Print a sorted list of all the records in a table/file including all the fields	Section 2 Task 2.12
5.3	Print a list of all records in a table/file matched by a single condition search	Section 3 Task 3.7
5.4	Print only selected fields from the records in a table/file.	Section 3 Task 3.11
5.5	Print a list of all records in a table/file matched by a single condition search, but including only selected fields from the records	Section 3 Task 3.12

Quick reference guide

Create a new database

Start Access. (Use Start button, All Programs, MS Access.)

Choose to create a blank Access database.
Enter the name, choose the folder, click Create. The database window appears.

Open an existing database

Either: Start Access. (Use Start button, All Programs, MS Access.) Choose to open a file from the list or select More Files.

In the Open dialogue box, find the file you want, click Open. The database window appears.

Or: Search in My Documents or its subfolders for the file you want. Double click on the file to start Access and open the file. The database window appears.

Create a database table

Write down the fields, types and lengths before you start. Have the database window open, Tables selected in the Objects list.

Double click Create table in Design view.

Enter field names and types in top of design window. For each field, enter size and any other details in lower half of window. F6 key swaps from upper to lower half and back.

Save design and give table a name. Do not create a primary key for Level 1.

Design view and Datasheet view

Tables and queries have both these views. Design view is for creating or altering the structure. Datasheet view is for entering or viewing data.

Swap between the views by using the left-most toolbar button or use the View menu.

Enter and edit data in a table

Do this in Datasheet view of a table.

Click into the field and key in the data. A record is automatically saved when you move out of it. Widen columns if necessary to show all the data.

Delete a record

Select the row.

Click Delete Record button on toolbar or use Edit menu and choose Delete Record. You will see a warning that the record will be deleted.

Add a record

Add new records at the bottom of the table.

Sort in table

(Quick and temporary – also see sorting in query)

Click in the field (column) you want to use for sorting. Click Sort Ascending or Sort Descending button on toolbar.

Print a table

Open the table in Datasheet view.

Preview first. (File, Print Preview or use Preview button.) Then File, Print.

To change to landscape, File, Page Setup, Page tab, click on Landscape, then OK. You have to do this every time – Access will not remember that you want landscape.

Print selected records	Open the table.
	Select the records. File, Print.
	Click Selected Records option button. OK.
Queries	Queries do not save data, but use data taken from tables. Use queries to sort records and to select records and fields for display.
Create a query	With the database window open, click Queries in the Objects list. Double click Create query in Design view. Add the table you need. Close the Show Table window.
	The lower part of the design window is the design grid where you set up the query. Put in the fields you want by dragging down from the table or double clicking.
Sorting	In the Sort row of the design grid, click in the field (column) you want to sort by. Choose ascending or descending from the drop down box.
Displaying or hiding fields	In each column of the design grid is a tick box. Tick to show the field, no tick to hide the field.
Selecting by one criterion	In the Criteria row of the design grid, click in the field you want to use. Type in your search criterion. This can be:
	The exact data entry you are looking, e.g. Oxford
	A criterion using relational operators, e.g. >10
	Relational operators are: > greater than, < less than, >= greater than or equal to, <= less than or equal to, = equal to, <> not equal to.
To see the query results	Change to Datasheet view by clicking the left-most toolbar button.
Save a query	Click the save button and give the query an informative name starting qry
Use an existing query	In the database window, with Queries Object selected, select the query. Either click Design to see Design view or click Open to see Datasheet view.
Changing a database structure	You can always add fields or increase field sizes. If you delete fields or reduce field sizes you are likely to lose data. Go to the Design view of a table to change its structure.
Close a database, table or query	File menu, choose Close.
Close Access	File menu, choose Exit.